Jackass in a Hailstorm

Adventures in Leadership Communication

Tim Hayes

ISBN: 1-4536-5888-2
ISBN-13: 9781453658888

To

Ellen Marie

TABLE OF CONTENTS

ACKNOWLEDGEMENTS

The lessons shared in this book were learned over the course of nearly 30 years in newspaper reporting, government public relations, corporate communications, agency work, and serving clients as a standalone communications consultant. There have been tremendous tutors along the way, and it is my pleasure to acknowledge a portion of them here.

My thanks go to: Randy Jesick, the best journalism professor I ever knew and who remains a friend to this day; Berry Lee, my first boss in public relations, whose sense of calm and gentle humor amid some of the craziest scenarios ever continues to inspire and instruct me; Dan McCarthy and David Osterhout, compatriots in corporate communications whose standards of excellence and hard work, balanced with a sense of mischief and fun, made life on the job such a blast; Dale Stetzer, who rescued me from looming unemployment and opened a window to a new world of big-scale events; the late Susan Bohn, who took a chance on "a writer who could learn banking;" the late Pat Capretto, whose Zen-like peace and astounding professional skill will always amaze me; Gladys Edmunds, who has been my "guardian angel" and coach; and Glen Meakem, whose story serves as a blueprint for entrepreneurs like me, and who has been enormously gracious with his time, his wisdom, and his radio microphone.

Special appreciation goes to Tim Wesley, my college roommate and best friend, whose steady shoulder and level head have been a welcome safe harbor for my entire adult life.

And most of all, I thank the good Lord for my parents, my two sisters, my three fantastic and talented and inspirational children, and of course my beautiful, loving, smart, funny, tough when she needs to be and tender when I need her to be, center of my universe—my wonderful wife, Ellen, without whom I am nowhere and nothing.

Finally, I thank you for allowing me to share my experiences in this book with you. There are lots more stories to write, so please let me know of any ideas and reactions to what you've read here. I look forward to continuing our dialogue.

FORWARD

By Glen Meakem
Co-Founder and Managing Director,
Meakem Becker Venture Capital,
Former Founder, Chairman and CEO, FreeMarkets Inc.

Leadership is communication.

There's no other way to say it, because it's the truth.

I believe it from first-hand experience leading people in military, corporate, entrepreneurial, and community environments. My friend Tim Hayes believes it from first-hand experience on the other side, the strategic and tactical communications support side, where he's distinguished himself over the years as a trusted counselor and writer to CEOs and other types of leaders.

The stories in this book stand up, since they're based on actual situations and astute observations. People are people, and they don't always make great decisions. But when they do, the results speak for themselves and the people responsible can shine. When those people are charged with leading individuals and organizations, solid communication skills more often than not serve as tie-breakers and difference-makers.

I went to Harvard College on a military scholarship and after serving as an officer in the United States Army Reserve and working in marketing for Kraft Foods, I returned to Harvard for my MBA. While I was studying at Harvard, Saddam Hussein invaded Kuwait and I volunteered and ended up serving as a combat engineer platoon leader in the 1991 Gulf War. While my upbringing and early leadership experiences in school and in sports certainly taught me the importance of leaders making their wishes clear and setting expectations, believe me, there's nothing like serving as an Army officer in a war zone to snap those lessons into sharp practice.

After completing my MBA and working as a consultant with McKinsey & Company and a Manager at General Electric, I came up with an idea to use the Internet to automate and improve the purchasing function of major corporations. So as the new economy took shape in the mid-1990s, I founded and served as Chairman and Chief Executive Officer of FreeMarkets, Inc., a leading business-to-business Internet company. My team and I at FreeMarkets had truly breakthrough ideas and technology, but navigating the start-up phase, followed quickly by the Internet Bubble and then the Internet Bust, proved to be highly challenging. As my company's leader, I had to set clear points on the horizon—clear targets—toward which everyone in my growing organization could navigate. Had I failed to do this consistently and clearly, we would have been one of the many companies in that era that failed, instead of one of the few that survived and thrived.

Leadership is communication. I believe much of the success of FreeMarkets, which my team and I took public five years after I founded it and then sold for $500 million five years after that, stemmed from regular, credible, and trustworthy dialogue among all leaders and all employees.

Today, I direct my attention and energies toward helping new entrepreneurs through Meakem Becker Venture Capital, and on promoting pro-growth, pro-freedom policies and plans through my weekly radio show, *The Glen Meakem Program*. Yet my mantra remains the same. When people know where they're going, and why, and what is expected of them along the way, results lean more heavily and reliably toward success. It's all about communication.

When Tim and I first began working together, he told me point blank that I could do better as a public speaker. Truth is, I thought I was pretty good. After all, I had led soldiers in a combat zone and taken a company public. Speaking to groups—even large audiences—was not something that scared me. But as I listened to Tim's observations and recommendations for improvement, they were so filled with common sense and so grounded in Tim's real-life experience dealing with other leaders over the course of his decorated career, that I put them into practice immediately. He was right. I could do better and I have.

That same sense of easy-going, entertaining, conversational and practical instruction based on firmly grounded expertise comes through on every page of this book. But that's no surprise. That's Tim's style. I'm happy he's put this collection of essays together, because they prove, over and over, the one truth that he and I both know in our bones.

Leadership is communication.

INTRODUCTION

Big Bird is really a dragon.

No, it's true. In the 1950s, Jim Henson created a seven-foot tall marionette/puppet dragon character controlled by a person inside the costume. The dragon hawked La Choy Chinese food on television.

A few years later, as Henson joined the team of educators, child psychologists, and writers developing a radically new TV show for preschoolers called *Sesame Street*, it became clear during some initial testing that a bridge between the fanciful world of the Muppets and the gritty real-life world of the city-street set was needed to hold kids' attention.

Big Bird—the retooled chop suey television pitch-dragon— became that bridge, and the rest is history.

It's one of the lesser-known examples of taking something created for one purpose and reimagining it to perform an entirely different function. This book is another example of that transformational dynamic at work.

The essays that make up each chapter here first were written as regular blog postings on my firm's website over the course of 12 months from July 2009 to June 2010. As a seasoned communications consultant who has worked with top executives from companies ranging from the ranks of the Fortune 100 to the most modest, but high-energy technology startups, I wrote these blogs to share my thoughts, perspectives, and ideas on what constitutes effective leadership communications.

Starting from a loyal band of fans and expanding to a worldwide audience, these blogs have helped me gain an even deeper appreciation of the practice of leadership communication from new friends as near as the next zip code and as far as Australia, London, Japan, and Abu Dubai.

The title "Jackass in a Hailstorm" comes from one of the essays in the book, but in a larger sense it describes the effect of leadership communications done poorly. Everything I write in the pages to follow is meant to help leaders avoid being caught in a situation where their communications efforts have been so lacking that they're left with no other option but to just stand there and take the abuse they've earned—like a jackass in a hailstorm.

Fortunately, most of the leaders with whom I've had the honor of working knew enough to listen to expert counsel and make the right moves to handle issues before they became problems. Notice I said "most." Some of the ones who did not served as the basis for a few of the stories shared in this volume.

My goal is always to entertain, enlighten, inform, instruct, and hold myself up for well-deserved ridicule occasionally. It is my deepest hope that you find the stories here illuminating and thought-provoking, even as they elicit a chuckle every now and again. For a deeper understanding and exploration of the concepts introduced throughout the book, a series of Discussion Prompts appears after each essay.

Effective leadership communication does not get the proper level of study or practical feedback as individuals are trained along their professional career paths. Yet I can think of few leadership attributes more worthy of continuous, comprehensive attention. So much rides on how well leaders share their vision and passion with the people they wish to lead. So much can be lost when leaders don't communicate well. So much can be achieved when the opposite occurs.

Don't be a jackass in a hailstorm. Your people will respect you more and follow you more fervently. Read on, and see.

Tim Hayes
June 2010

Chapter 1
LEADERSHIP

Climbing the ladder of organizational success isn't easy. For those who make it to the top, or close to the top, much is expected. Make your numbers each quarter, keep expenses controlled, manage to maximum productivity and profitability. That's what makes the world of business go 'round, and there's nothing wrong with any of it.

At the same time, though, having the big title doesn't necessarily make one a true leader. Employees, staff members, direct reports—whatever label you prefer—may listen to the person out front, but that doesn't mean they are true followers. Yet to be a true leader, one must have true followers.

To effectively lead and be perceived as a true leader, communications must be part of the management mix. No, strike that—communications shouldn't be just one part of the mix; it must be the underpinning, the foundation, the bedrock supporting every single part of the mix.

Answer these questions honestly:

- Do you know where you're taking your people?
- Do your people know where you're taking them?
- Do they believe it?
- Do they believe that *you* believe it?
- Do they understand their role?
- Do they understand *your* role?
- Do they believe that you are working with their best interest front and center, even as you all are working to advance the organization's growth?

If the answer to any of these questions is "no," then you may be a manager but you're not a true leader. And in today's versatile, volatile economy and workforce, you need to bring more to your role. You indeed can be a leader, a true leader, through effective communications practiced consistently and wholeheartedly.

The stories in this chapter—the largest and most important in the entire book—convey some humorous and pragmatic lessons about achieving that critical goal of powerful, practical, and ultimately profitable leadership communications.

1.1
Dr. Pratt's Morning Stroll
The Big Idea: Leaders should be visible.

Each morning, as the sun tried to push through the watery cloudiness that stubbornly enveloped the sloping hills of Indiana, Pennsylvania, Dr. Willis Pratt stepped out of his flat and went for a stroll.

Usually with a member of the maintenance crew in tow, Dr. Pratt made his way across the campus of Indiana University of Pennsylvania—or IUP, my alma mater, and the school where he served as president from the mid-1940s through the late '60s—each dawn. He'd point out places where a sidewalk may have begun to crack, or some hedges needed trimming, or a fresh coat of paint or spit-shine would make a building look a bit better. The maintenance fellow would take diligent notes and those projects would help fill his day.

But Dr. Pratt knew something else was happening as he took his daily walk through his beloved university. He would stop and talk with students on their way to their early morning classes. He got to know their names and their aspirations, and vice versa. He shared his love of the school, its grounds, and its people on a one-to-one basis. He became the tangible personification of IUP, and the genuine affection and respect he received from the student body turned into lasting support for the university as those students became alumni.

And all because he steadfastly went for a morning walk every day. How different from so many of today's leaders, who take private elevators to their top-floor corner offices, who are never—ever—seen simply strolling the hallways and cafeterias of their buildings, and who seemingly abhor the prospect of actually engaging in casual conversation with their employees that's not scripted or pre-scheduled eight weeks in advance.

Some years ago, the Corporate Communications Department of the large company where I was working asked me to coordinate a series of "walking tours" for the CEO, where he would visit with a work group, chat with their employees, share his vision for the corporation, and generate some needed rapport with the frontline troops, as it were. As feared, however, these visits morphed from their stated team-building intent into high-stress, high-stakes inspections and tests of how well the department being visited could ramp up an impressive show-and-tell for the Big Cheese. Instead of groups clamoring to be included on the list, they sprinted in the opposite direction and looked for a place to hide. Not exactly the outcome we were shooting for.

It quickly became apparent that you can't schedule spontaneity or demand an open spirit of dialogue and idea sharing. The "walking tours" met an early demise and were never resurrected. The lines of communication in the best organizations encompass both verbal and non-verbal channels, and we learned that our enterprise wasn't there quite yet.

In contrast, the students at IUP all those years ago knew Dr. Pratt. They saw him every day. They knew he wanted to be a part of their collegiate lives. He wasn't holed up in his office, appearing only for pre-staged photo ops or scripted presentations. They knew they could talk with him, whether in the Oak Grove at the center of campus, in his office in the main administration building, or at his on-campus home.

Can the leaders we know today say the same? Yes, security and safety are legitimate concerns. A CEO is a high-value asset that must be protected. But protecting doesn't have to mean precluding. Engendering trust and esprit de corps forms the foundation for effective leadership communication. And one of the best ways to achieve that as a leader is to simply permit yourself to be seen and approachable on a regular basis. Just like Dr. Pratt.

Discussion Prompts:

1.   **Why is a CEO's visibility worth so much?**

2. How would you overcome the problems with the "walking tours" mentioned in this essay?
3. List five more communications initiatives to support a CEO's heightened visibility.

1.2
Am I Speaking English?
The Big Idea: Do what you say you will do.

After a very enjoyable and productive week in Texas on a client assignment, I looked out the window of the plane as it landed in Pittsburgh to see a heavy snowfall well under way. Back in my car, I began the slippery, slow drive back to my home, about 30 miles off. But about halfway there, traffic came to a dead stop.

In my headlights stood a Pennsylvania State Trooper, forcefully instructing a state highway snowplow driver to run his truck up and down a two-mile hill that had become treacherous. The trooper would hold traffic at the foot of the hill while the plow cleared the slope for safe passage. So away went the truck, lights flashing, plow plowing, off into the winter's night.

And he never returned. An hour later, we hadn't moved and about five more inches of snow had piled up on the hill before us.

It reminded me of a cranky, terribly funny, great old lady I used to work across from 20 years ago named Olga. She ran the books for the Corporate Communications Department and took no guff from anybody, even the executives. When someone would give her an uninformed answer, or plead ignorance on an expense report, or say or do anything she deemed stupid or spineless, she had a pat response that would end the discussion instantly. Crusty old Olga would look the poor sap in the eye and ask, the sarcasm dripping from her tobacco-damaged larynx, "Am I speaking English?"

You can take university courses in ethics. You can study the titans of Greek philosophy. You can go to self-help seminars or order CDs on late-night TV infomercials. But I can save you a lot of time and money with a simple, foolproof, never-been-known-to-fail standard: Do what you say you will do.

How many millions of executives, politicians, celebrities, spouses, school children, employees, friends, you name it, have learned this the hard way—occasionally with disastrous economic, social, career- or relationship-busting results?

As professional communicators, the lesson for me and my counterparts remains taking our roles as the "Jiminy Crickets"—otherwise known as the consciences—of our organizations very seriously. Carefully consider what's being promised in a speech or news release. Ask the uncomfortable questions internally. Can we live up to what's being said? If not, how can we restate our position to avoid that negative feedback?

It's easy to always say the right thing. It's hard to always do it. But your character, credibility, and reputation rest on those two concepts matching up at all times.

That snowplow driver endangered the lives of thousands of commuters the other night by saying he'd do one thing and doing something else. I eventually made it up that hill, as did most drivers. But as my little sedan dug in and continued its climb, I kept wishing for one thing—to have been there when the State Trooper finally found that guy again. "Am I speaking English?" would be the kindest thing he'd say, I'm guessing.

Discussion Prompts:

1. How did you react to the concept of communications experts serving as the "conscience" of their organizations?
2. Is that a fair responsibility to assign a person in that position?
3. What would such an unspoken yet understood assignment mean to you?
4. How would you carry it out?

1.3
Potentially Ugly, Sometimes Necessary
The Big Idea: Don't fear honest evaluation.

The past winter here in the Northeast delivered sucker punch after sucker punch. We soldiered on under record snowfalls that made transportation difficult, tempers short, and electricity iffy.

The local utility company tells us that the power interruptions could have and would have been worse if they didn't maintain their policy of tree trimming to keep the electrical lines clear from falling trees and snapping branches. Having worked for an electric company somewhere in my hazy past, I know this to be true.

But that truth doesn't make the effects of the policy any easier on the eyes.

Now that the snow is gone and we're enjoying lovely springtime sunshine again, a brisk walk down our cul-de-sac or a brief drive to the store for a quart of milk reveals the aesthetic assault on our arboreal friends. The power lines are clear, all right, but in the process of clearing them, the trees look like they've been wildly hacked willy-nilly with little consideration to how they might appear.

It only goes to show that life poses choices like this all the time. Do you want things to work good or look good? Sometimes to do the necessary, you must accommodate the ugly.

In the world of leadership communications, the choice can come in a variety of forms and situations. Do you continue with traditional communications vehicles like newsletters or face-to-face meetings or electronic bulletin notices because they're traditional—or do you have the courage to learn about their true effectiveness and make changes where necessary in content, format, or timing? Do you offer relentless, context-free, even misleading cheerleading to your employees, even when things aren't going well—or do you tell the truth, followed by a positive message about plans to make the situation better?

The Enron story remains a classic case of communications gone haywire in the face of imminent disaster. The energy-trading house of cards was destined to collapse and the leadership team there knew it long before the actual implosion occurred. Yet they felt compelled to keep the illusion going—and not only going, but embellishing it every quarter to keep the stock price up, investor confidence high, and employee morale strong. When reality kicked in the front door and the inevitable happened, it only made the ruse and the accompanying sense of betrayal that much more embarrassing and painful.

People can forgive just about anything but a liar.

That's why it's better, when there's pain, to deal with it sooner rather than later. My three rules of great leadership communications still apply—promote the good, admit the bad, and explain improvements. It's not always easy and it can get ugly, but sometimes it's necessary in order to survive and move on as a leader.

Discussion Prompts:

1. **Leaders need to be positive. They also need to be truthful. Can you cite an example of a CEO who had to choose one or the other?**
2. **What were the effects on the reputations of him- or herself and the organization?**
3. **Why would a leadership team, like the one at Enron, keep up an illusion when they know it couldn't last?**
4. **If you were part of that leadership team, what would you have done?**

1.4
The CEO as Transformational Storyteller
The Big Idea: People may hear facts, but they listen to stories.

Amid economic challenges like those at work today, companies need to transform themselves, adapting to survive and even move ahead. But given the volume of coverage and advisory-oriented information out there, surprisingly little attention is paid to the role of one important person—the CEO. What can this key leader do?

According to a recent article in the McKinsey Quarterly, issued by management consultants McKinsey & Company, the first thing CEOs should do is something I agree with a thousand percent. CEOs must make their organization's transformation meaningful by making it personal, and they should do that through storytelling.

"People will go to extraordinary lengths for causes they believe in, and a powerful transformation story will create and reinforce their commitment. The ultimate impact of the story depends on the CEO's willingness to make the transformation personal, to engage others openly, and to spotlight successes as they emerge," say the experts at McKinsey, and they're right.

I wrote a speech for a client some time ago that proves the point. This gentleman had been named CEO of a company he had worked for all his life, succeeding a much younger man who had been brought in from the outside but who had passed away quite unexpectedly. While the younger CEO had done a fine job improving efficiency and shareholder returns, he lacked interpersonal skills and internal morale had suffered.

The new CEO, conversely, having been such an old hand within the company, was well-known and even more well-loved. He believed—truly believed—that when people came first, business results would follow. And that message served as the central theme of the speech I wrote for him, as he addressed all employees as his first act as CEO.

He told stories drawn from the people who mentored him as a young man, those who worked alongside him, those who inspired him, and those who came to look up to him over time. He tied these wonderful, warm stories to his vision of where he wanted the company to go. He told the people of the organization he now led that he needed them to believe in each other the way he always believed in them.

And by the time he was finished, every one of those 2,400 people—whether they were in the same building, or watching via video across the company footprint—would have run through a brick wall for him.

He made the transformation personal through heartfelt stories. There's no reason that CEOs in any organization, regardless of the challenges they face, can't achieve the necessary transformations the same way. It can't be faked. It can't be half-hearted. But when it's done well, it can't be denied. A great speech delivered with conviction can transform people and organizations.

Discussion Prompts:

1.   Why would a CEO need to be a good storyteller?
2.   How could business schools and other training sources help future leaders improve their skills in this area?
3.   Cite an example, either recently or from the past, where a CEO succeeded or failed as a storyteller—and the resulting ramifications.

1.5
Doing Solitary in the Corner Office
The Big Idea: Rigid chains of command stifle healthy dialogue.

Many years ago, when I was a PR greenhorn at a large corporation, I had returned from an assignment at a field office and approached the first floor elevators to get back to my little cubicle. Ahead of me walked the CEO of the company, headed for the same elevators. What happened next still confounds me, more than 20 years later.

The CEO had pressed the call button and caught sight of me as the doors opened and he entered the car. I was far enough away that I had to jog to make it into the same car, but as I got close enough to hop in, I could see the toes of his shiny polished wingtips parallel to the doors, which were closing on me. I could also hear the repeated pressing of a button from inside the car.

All I could deduce was that the CEO had forced himself into a corner of the elevator far enough that he didn't have to see or acknowledge or, heaven forbid, talk with anyone—especially an employee!...the horror!—and that he was frantically hitting the "Close Door" button to make his solitary escape to the executive floor.

Now understand, this man was intellectually brilliant. He held degrees in engineering and law. The board of directors brought him in to steer the company through an aggressive period of growth and deregulation. Yet his interpersonal skills were absolutely awful, and his leadership suffered as a result.

Another surreal example. I had to interview the CEO for an employee magazine story. First, I got reprimanded for calling his assistant myself. Then, the Corporate Communications department head insisted he accompany me to the interview. But the topper came as the three of us sat at a conference table in the CEO's office.

I asked my first question, looking directly at the CEO who was, after all, the subject of the story. This, I learned after a few extremely awkward moments, simply would not do. That's when my department head whispered to me, "Tim, ask me the questions." And that's how the rest of the meeting went. I'd ask my department head the question, he'd repeat it to the CEO, the CEO would answer the department head, I'd scribble the answers, and we'd start this bizzaro merry-go-round all over again with the next question. Keep in mind, we were all of three feet apart from each other.

Good grief, there's chain of command and then there's a chain of fools, and I felt ensnared by both that afternoon. I'd assume the CEO simply didn't like me personally, if not for the fact that everyone else in my department had a similar story or two.

The point here is that great leaders have the expertise, knowledge, strategic and analytical powers to set a bold course for their organizations—plus the engaging, affable, inclusive, genuine feel for the people they lead. It's not the easiest thing in the world to do, I know, having suffered from jitters making small talk with strangers at professional gatherings and receptions for years.

The fact remains, though, that I'd rather have a leader who's great with people over one with a preponderance for book-smarts. Leaders with people-smarts have followers who believe in and act on the vision, not simply understand it. And therein lies all the difference.

Discussion Prompts:

1. What do you think—is it more important for a leader to be brilliant or to be approachable and engaging? Why?
2. Why do you think a CEO might feel uncomfortable around his or her employees?
3. How would you advise such a leader in terms of enhancing his or her standing with employees?

1.6
Red-Handed, Red-Faced? Ready to Lead
The Big Idea: People will forgive honest and sincere repentance.

She was busted, and she knew it. I had her dead to rights. One of my daughters, maybe three years old at the time, with her hand literally in the cookie jar. So I removed the treat from her little fist, sat her on my fatherly lap, and asked if she wanted to tell me anything.

"Yes, Daddy," she said, her wide green eyes peering remorsefully up at me. "Can I have my cookie back now?"

Art Linkletter, wherever you are today, you were right. Kids do say the darndest things. What's weird sometimes, though, is that some of the brightest, most savvy adults in the business world—when they get caught with their hand in the cookie jar—can be just as defiant as a three-year-old who wants that damn cookie back.

As a professional consultant and writer to CEOs and other leaders, I am occasionally left slack-jawed, flat-footed, and dumbfounded by how obtuse such otherwise smart and admirable individuals can be in these situations. My advice is always to tell the truth—and to be the first one to tell it, before others can establish a baseline narrative that forces my client into a reactive stance. Mom was right, the truth will always come out, and if it's different than what she heard in the first place? Oooo, there's a world'a hurt comin' your way, Bubba.

Leaders like to be admired and emulated. Honesty, trust, and credibility form the foundation. Ethics, wisdom, courage, and humility build the structure. A leader shooting for a bronze bust tomorrow but who has clay feet today won't make it. When you're not structurally sound in the eyes of those looking to you for leadership, sooner or later things will go south—hard, fast, and ugly.

I have known business leaders with intimidating top-floor corner offices who got caught in peccadilloes, running shady books, and other such malfeasance. A handful bullied their way back to pre-eminence through sheer force of personality, intimidation, and other behavior roughly equivalent to stocking the castle moat with hungry alligators. So that method can work, I suppose.

But the ones who took to heart the quaint, crocheted, Whitman's Sampler wisdom of honesty indeed being the best policy usually came out of their firestorm better people and better leaders. They had proven themselves worthy of their position by admitting their mistake, apologizing for it, and establishing a road back.

They may not have always kept the corner office (although most did, by the way), but at least they could live with the reflection in the mirror every morning. And in my book, that's a higher victory than crouching behind a parapet, clutching onto a great title, yet having no supporters, believers, or friends.

Discussion Prompts:

1. Give at least two examples of leaders whose first instinct was to cover up the problem—then describe the fallout of that decision, both personally and professionally.
2. If you were the communications advisor to a CEO or other leader, how would you go about steering your client during a crisis—especially when the truth could bring additional short-term heat?

1.7
Ringo, the Luckiest Man on Earth
The Big Idea: Preparation lets you make the most of opportunities.

I don't believe in coincidence. I think everything happens for a reason, even though we may not realize it as it's happening. Instead, I believe in luck—as defined by that first century Roman gadfly Seneca, who said, "Luck is what happens when preparation meets opportunity."

Using Seneca's definition, I would have to say that the luckiest man on the face of the earth—with apologies to Lou Gehrig in "Pride of the Yankees"—has to be one Richard Starkey of Liverpool, England. You may know him by his stage name, Ringo Starr.

John Lennon, Paul McCartney, and George Harrison had been playing rock-and-roll music together as the Quarrymen and eventually the Beatles for a couple of years since meeting as high schoolers. They'd had a handful of drummers, the most recent a nice-enough chap by the name of Pete Best, whose Mum had helped book gigs for the boys. But going into their first recording sessions, the lads heard that they'd have to use a studio-employed drummer. Pete's beats were lacking. He had to go.

And then, just weeks before their first major live performance in September 1962—the one that rocketed them to stardom—the Beatles poached Ringo from a band led by Rory Storm, whoever that was. Instantly, the serendipitous Mr. Starkey punched a ticket to ride the gravy train to musical, cultural, and financial heights few have experienced.

But was it luck alone? No, it was preparation (Ringo was clearly a better, more experienced drummer who could come up with unusual and distinct rhythmic approaches) coupled with opportunity (the boys needed a replacement in a hurry).

What does all this have to do with leadership communication? Plenty. In fact, it has everything to do with it.

Identifying and articulating a vision provides the foundation for leadership communication. But what happens when challenges, competitors, disasters, distractions, detractors, and various other forms of negative influencers converge? Leaders need to be prepared in these instances, too.

For example, is BP simply having a run of bad luck? What about Toyota a few months ago? No, they were not properly prepared to react when the opportunity arose to openly, honestly, and courageously address their respective crises. Just ask their CEOs whether they're feeling lucky lately.

Handling crises may be the most visible and tangible example of preparation meeting opportunity in leadership communications, but it's hardly the only one. How about seizing the imagination of the marketplace to elevate a product or image? Think of Lady Gaga's musical training at Julliard (yes, it's true) meeting her avant-garde sense of fashion and performance art. Or how about demonstrating patience and competence that outlasts less well-seasoned competitors? Think of IBM still standing, still growing, still relevant after Commodore, Compaq, Atari and so many other computing companies wilted in the competitive heat.

I believe in luck. Maybe more accurately, I believe in making your own luck through preparation that can capitalize on opportunities as they arise. Hey, if nothing else, it sure worked for Ringo—the luckiest man on earth.

Discussion Prompts:

1. **Major corporations have contingency plans for everything, but can fall down when communicating during rapidly changing crises. What are some strategies they can always put into practice to avoid such pitfalls?**
2. **Describe a corporate example where preparation met opportunity to address a crisis with well-planned and well-executed communications.**

1.8
The Cowher 24-Hour Rule
The Big Idea: Keep victories and defeats in balance.

When my oldest daughter was in elementary school, she played soccer with the area youth league. One year I was pressed into service as her team's assistant coach, which really wasn't all that big of a deal, if it hadn't been for one parent.

One famous parent. One famous parent who also coached football, albeit the American version. You may have heard of him. His name was Bill Cowher. And this was circa 1998-99, while he was Head Coach of the NFL's Pittsburgh Steelers, before he became an in-studio analyst for CBS Sports.

Yeah, THAT Bill Cowher. The Jaw. The intense, driven, in-your-face, Super Bowl-winning motivator whose icy stare could burn through sheet metal. Yes, this was the lunatic who would stand on the sidelines while I was trying to get a bunch of silly, unfocused third-grade girls to run soccer plays. No pressure there, right?

But you want to know something? For as wild, severe, and passionate as Coach Cowher appeared on Sunday afternoon as he led my beloved Steelers, he was just another Dad on Saturday morning watching his little girl play soccer. He never said a word to me or the other coach about the games. People gave him his space, waited in line and chatted with him at the refreshment stand, helped him unload bottled waters and sliced oranges from his car when it was his family's turn to bring snacks. "Hey, Bill, how ya doin'?"

One story I heard about Coach Cowher and his wife, Kaye, some years later helped explain this seeming dichotomy. Bill and Kaye both played sports at North Carolina State, where they first met as students. As Cowher moved on to the NFL as a player, assistant coach, and eventually head coach, he and Kaye made a pact. They promised each other that after any major event—whether winning the Super Bowl, or losing it (both of which Cowher did while coaching the Steelers), or anything in between—the celebration or the despair could only last 24 hours. No exceptions.

You could set off fireworks, turn cartwheels, and pop champagne corks all you wanted, but for 24 hours only. You could throw rocks at empty beer cans or shout at life's indignities and unfairness until your throat was hoarse, but for 24 hours only. After the earth made one twirl on its axis, though, it was time to move on and get back to work.

After I heard about that agreement, it really made a lot of sense to me. It can take a long time and lot of hard work to get to a moment of truth. If you succeed, of course it's right and proper and deserving to celebrate. Conversely, if you fail, it's okay to feel bad and lick your wounds. Either way, you've earned as much.

But the Cowhers were on to something really smart. Neither the highs nor the lows can or should last indefinitely. Nobody likes an insufferable braggart or an unrelenting downer.

I can see this principle holding just as true in business, politics, academics, entertainment, or any other field you can think of, as it does in sports. I've had days of pure joy and pride in having accomplished something terrific, and I've had days I'd rather never think about again, thank you very much.

As with most things, it's a matter of keeping it all in balance. That's how the willful, forceful man who had led other willful, forceful men to two Super Bowls kept his cool on those dewy mornings watching our kids chase that crazy soccer ball around. It's a lesson I've never forgotten. Thanks, Coach.

Discussion Prompts:

1. **Why is limiting reaction to events, whether good or bad, important to effective leadership?**
2. **Should the same level of effort go into addressing and communicating bad news as is spent on good news? More? Less? Why?**

1.9
Mushroom Management Never Works
The Big Idea: If you value people, tell them.

Look, opinions are like belly-buttons—everybody's got one. Especially when it comes to managerial techniques. Loyal readers of this blog know that we try to concentrate on helping leaders do their jobs better by understanding and implementing solid communications practices.

So in that spirit, a recent Business Week article written by workplace consultant Liz Ryan caught my eye. Ryan lists a few less-than-stellar strategies deployed by far too many managers that only serve to drive great talent away. Two of Ryan's more potent observations hit home with me. Excerpts from her article are seen below, followed by my reflections.

Here's the first:
If you want to drive talented people away, don't tell them when they shine.
Fear of a high-self-esteem employee is prevalent among average-grade corporate leadership teams. Look how hard it is for so many managers to say, "Hey Bob, you did a great job today." Whatever the reason for silence, leaders who can't say, "Thanks—good going!" can plan on bidding farewell to their most able team members in short order.

Sad but true. We've all experienced this, I would guess. You complete a complex project with many moving parts; multiple constituencies to involve, engage, and motivate; and performance metrics to meet or exceed—and you do it—but with one minor aspect that perhaps didn't come off flawlessly, or that caused some self-important jerk to rat you out to the boss.

And that's all the boss remembers—the 0.1 percent that didn't work, not the 99.9 percent that did.

I once had a supervisor confront me with: "You know what your problem is?" "I have many problems," I replied. "Which one is bothering you right now?" Then he unloaded this gem on me: "You have an irrational need for external praise!" My retort? "That's because I don't get any praise internally." Not a month later, I had shaken the dust of that dysfunctional place off my feet, launched my independent consultancy, and have never looked back.

Here's another great observation by Ryan:
If you prefer a team of C-list players, keep employees in the dark.

Sharp knowledge workers want to know what's going on in their organizations, beyond their departmental silos. They want some visibility into the company's plans and their own career mobility. Leaders who can't stand to shine a light on their firms' goals, strategies, and systems are all but guaranteed to spend a lot of money running ads on Monster.com.

This is basic PR 101. People will fill in the blanks, connect the dots, paint the picture, play the music—whatever cliché you like best—whether they have the correct and complete information or not. Isn't it better to provide them with the right information, so that everyone's operating from the same playbook? Duh.

I suppose insecure managers twist the old chestnut that "Knowledge Is Power" into such a pretzel that only by hoarding knowledge do they believe they can retain their power. But guess what, Sherlock? When your staff underperforms based on your sorry communication record, who looks bad? (*Psst! The correct answer is:* **You**.) Double duh.

Employees resent being treated like mushrooms—constantly kept in the dark, as dung is dumped on them. That's why some studies suggest that, as the economic recovery continues, the best people will be heading for the exits seeking greener pastures. And nowhere will this be more true than where they unfortunately labor under the thumbs of managers who can't, or won't, communicate effectively.

Discussion Prompts:

1. Basic communications with people pays steady dividends, but many managers cannot bring themselves to practice it. How would you help foster a more open environment for communications within your work group?
2. How would you help foster greater two-way communication?

1.10
This Too Shall Pass

The Big Idea: If you want people to embrace change, live the change yourself.

Over the course of nearly 20 years in corporate and government communications, and 10 years as an independent consultant, I've been in the room many times when the Big Idea gets hatched.

"We need to change the culture of this organization!" "We're going to do things differently around here to serve our customers better!" "Our employees will embrace this change and behave differently from now on!"

All noble, even necessary, ideals. Fortunes are made and lost on how well those lofty goals are met. Yet without one key ingredient, you might as well declare, "We're flying to the moon tomorrow in a magic Yugo!" because the level of credibility and sustainability would be just about the same.

Culture change—asking employees to think and act in sometimes radically different ways forevermore—is hard. People don't like to think about it, let alone be told they've got to do it, starting on Monday. As one curmudgeonly friend of mine (a longtime veteran at a former employer that shall remain nameless) used to say, when a new Employee Program Du Jour would roll around: "This too shall pass."

I was in my early 30s then, and even at that relatively tender professional age, I found his eye-rolling, sigh-laden, wizened sense of resignation, summed up in that simple sentence, alarmingly cynical and negative. What hurt, though, was the fact that either my co-workers in Corporate Communications—or worse, I—had helped develop the very messages being met with such scoffing resistance. What hurt more was that he was, all too often, correct.

Yet I also have seen culture change actually embraced and executed well within organizations. It can work, and when it does it creates profound and positive improvement. Employee satisfaction rises, which paves the way for greater customer satisfaction, which leads to increased loyalty, higher sales and revenues, stronger financial performance, and a complete win for all parties involved. A rising tide indeed lifts all boats. But again, when it comes to these types of initiatives, one key ingredient must be perpetually present, personally promoted, and powerfully perceived.

All the expert communications support available won't cut it without this single ingredient. There are precious few ways to force this ingredient to present itself—it must come organically to have any real or lasting impact.

So, what is this essential ingredient? It is the belief, commitment, involvement, and engagement—truly held, honestly promoted, credibly demonstrated, and enthusiastically shared—by the very top leaders of the organization. Employees can smell a lack of sincerity a mile away, and while they may have an "Employee of the Month" smile pasted across their faces, on the inside they're thinking, "This too shall pass."

Where I've seen culture change take root and lead to growth and success, leaders have done their jobs and provided leadership. They have spent the mental energy to realize that their organizations can—and should, and must—do better. They are the ones who spearhead the charge, gathering research and documentation to understand the situation and then pushing and prodding their teams to help identify fresh ways to make it better. They carry the message forward, with purpose, confidence, and clarity. They lead the change by living the change. They tolerate no B.S., especially from the person they see in the mirror.

To be leader requires having followers. To gather followers, one must offer a clear vision and be willing to actively participate in its execution. Expertly developed communication, driven by clear and consistent messaging delivered in ways that employees accept, provides the undergirding to a leader's culture change initiative.

But the initiative's ultimate success or failure—whether it too shall pass, or whether it shall remain and truly become embedded in the culture of the organization—rests with how strongly employees believe that their leaders believe what's being said.

Discussion Prompts:

1. Why are employees resistant to change—even change that will make their jobs and their organization better?
2. How can proper messaging overcome this resistance?
3. Develop a communications plan to address a major change (real or fictional) at your organization.

1.11
When the Defecation Hits the Ventilation
The Big Idea: Loyalty has a breaking point.

America is the land of second chances. Just ask Bill Clinton, Martha Stewart, David Letterman, Robert Downey Jr., or a thousand other examples. But when high-profile people abuse the reservoir of public goodwill, things can get a little more difficult.

We have a situation like this in my hometown of Pittsburgh right now, featuring the star quarterback of the Steelers, Ben Roethlisberger. In 2006, he suffered a number of injuries after crashing his motorcycle—injuries that would likely have been less serious had he been wearing a helmet. In 2008, a woman filed a lawsuit alleging that Roethlisberger sexually assaulted her in a Lake Tahoe hotel room, and last week, another woman alleged that Roethlisberger sexually assaulted her in a night club outside of Atlanta.

This is a 28-year-old man who earns more than $100 million playing football—something at which there can be absolutely no question he does extremely well, with guts, smarts, an iron-clad abhorrence toward losing, and two Super Bowl championships in four years. He is the "face" of the Pittsburgh Steelers, a storied franchise that since its inception has been owned by the Rooney family—legends in the world of professional sports who are revered in Pittsburgh for doing things right, with pride, respect for others, and a sense of fairness at all times.

Steeler Nation—the fan base that begins in Pittsburgh and reaches around the world—"bleeds black and gold" and supports the team in good years and bad. Ben Roethlisberger is the willing recipient of much of that love.

But he may have pushed his luck too far this time. You can be a great football player and a complete knucklehead off the field. Sports lore is chock full of brilliant athletes who behave like idiots in real life. Sometimes it's endearing, sometimes it's easy to shrug off. Then there are times like this.

It's important to note that nothing has been proven in the Lake Tahoe case, and charges haven't even been filed in the Georgia incident. Roethlisberger is presumed innocent until proven guilty in the eyes of the law. But I'm not talking about the law, I'm talking about using up goodwill and straining the limits of what your fan base will tolerate. Nothing good happens at 2 a.m., I don't care how many Super Bowl rings you have.

The situation reminds me of what a high school social studies teacher used to say when the class would get to the point in a story from history where a tyrant gets his comeuppance or an event triggers a population to revolt. He'd stop, pause, look at the room full of students and say, "And that, ladies and gentlemen, is where the defecation hit the ventilation." (Think about it...it will come to you...got it? Okay, let's move on.)

His point was, people's willingness to put up with unacceptable, offensive, or disappointing behavior is finite. This goes for political leaders, CEOs, entertainers, and as Mr. Roethlisberger may be about to learn the hard way, athletes.

A big part of leadership—and that includes being elevated to the forefront of your chosen profession—entails not regularly entering situations where you can end up looking like a jackass, or worse. (Are you listening, Kanye?) Even if Big Ben escapes these episodes legally, he would be well-served to take a good long look in the mirror and grow up. He's had his second, third, and fourth chances already. There's not much time left on the clock.

Discussion Prompts:

1. As a professional communications expert, how would you have counseled Ben Roethlisberger in this instance?
2. How would you have counseled the Steelers? The National Football League?
3. What would you do if all the attorneys affiliated with this case told everyone involved to say nothing?

❖ ❖ ❖

1.12
No One Will Ever Know
The Big Idea: Social media has changed the rules of image control.

By now, you've probably heard about the embarrassing faux pas committed by NBC's Ann Curry, whose commencement address last week to Wheaton College in Massachusetts included kudos to famous alumni such as the Rev. Billy Graham, former House Speaker Dennis Hastert and horror movie director Wes Craven—the only problem being that those folks attended Wheaton College in Illinois.

To her credit, Curry posted an apology on the college's website, saying, "I am mortified by my mistake, and can only hope the purity of my motive, to find a way to connect with the graduates and to encourage them to a life of service, will allow you to forgive me."

But the most disturbing aspect of this episode—to me, anyway—came when the school posted a video of Curry's address but edited out the parts where she cited the erroneous alumni names.

Wheaton College—please—drag yourself into the '90s! What in the world were those administrators thinking? Imagine the president, the trustee chairman, and head of public relations hunkered down in the Situation Room, deep within the bowels of the main administration building. Did the dialogue sound like this?

President: "We have a problem here, boys. A terrible, terrible problem."
Trustee: "Oh, it's a stinker, all right."
PR Guy: "What problem? That thing with Curry getting her names mixed up?"
President: "Well, what else?!"
Trustee: "Oh, this is quite a pickle."
President: "We have to erase any evidence that it ever happened!"

Trustee: "Erasing's good."

PR Guy: "You're kidding, of course."

President: "I most certainly am not kidding! This never happened! We must expunge all record of it and you are to deny it to the media."

Trustee: "No one can ever know."

President: "No one will ever know."

PR Guy: "There were hundreds of graduates and their parents there—each with cell phones and video recorders! It was probably on YouTube before Curry sat down!"

President (hands over his ears): "Lalalalalalala! I can't hear you!"

There are no secrets any longer. Everyone is a potential journalist—muckraking, perhaps, but still a journalist. Embarrassing, unethical, even illegal behavior captured via camera phone or pocket video camera blankets the planet in seconds. YouTube is a wondrous thing, but its power must be respected.

Those in leadership positions must never assume that they can control any part of what they say or do in public—or even in private. Anything and everything is a heartbeat away from becoming public knowledge. And once it's online, it's eternal.

I'm sure Curry was sincere in her apology, and she deserves credit for admitting the sloppy research and taking responsibility. If only more high-profile people had the same instincts. The difference was that she knew that coming clean quickly was the only option—because her job is reporting on the follies of people who foolishly think they can still control events in this rapid-fire media world. The leaders at Wheaton College have much to learn from their commencement speaker, mistakes and all.

Discussion Prompts:

1. **Cite three ways that social media could enhance the accurate and positive information flow of an organization.**

2.   If you were Ann Curry, what else would you have done to recover from your mistake?

3.   What communications tactics can be deployed after an embarrassing event goes online?

1.13
In Praise of the Active Combatant
The Big Idea: Leaders must get directly involved in the vision they promote.

In today's business world, CEOs can't be spectators, but must be active combatants using effective communications as their most trusted tool.

Leadership by example is the only way that organizations can find clarity, direction, inspiration, and the sheer will to fight their way out of the economic fix they're in these days. And that responsibility falls squarely on the CEO. Just ask John Chambers, CEO of Cisco Systems.

"I'm the roadblock. In command and control, the enabler is the CEO," said Chambers in a recent interview with McKinsey & Company. "Part of it is the ability to paint a picture of what's possible…You've got to communicate, communicate, communicate…And the leader has to not only say the talk, she or he has got to walk the talk. Got to be the best example."

At issue, though, is a simple fact of human nature—people can't follow a vision they can't see, don't understand, or one that has not been conveyed to them with power, persuasiveness, and passion.

Earlier in my career, I served as the communications liaison for the CEO of a major financial services provider. He had assumed the office following the long tenure of a man who had quite dramatically and effectively rescued this company from liquidation some years before. But by the time he retired, the company had become stale and set in its ways. The new CEO planned to set a fresh course to keep the enterprise vibrant and growing in what had become a new competitive landscape.

I advised him that if he were the only person in the company who really "got" this new vision, then he'd be the only one working to carry it out. So we set out to capture the main elements of the vision, develop key message points that everyone from executives in the C-suite to tellers on the front lines could easily grasp, and push the information out into the company with vigor and enthusiasm.

And the guy most visible—through speeches to employee groups, customer gatherings, and investor conferences, along with a dedicated internal website and many other communications tools—was the CEO.

A spectator? Never. An active combatant? Always. Effective communications that took his vision and made it understandable and actionable to everyone in the company made a real difference.

Discussion Prompts:

1. Leaders must walk a fine line between visible, active leadership and crossing into a cult of personality. Cite examples of leaders who fulfilled that role without crossing the line.
2. How would you define when a CEO has let personality get the better of him or her?
3. Discuss an example of what happens to the organization, and what communications challenges are created, when a CEO goes too far?

1.14
Man Up, Mr. President
The Big Idea: Speaking only to supporters does not a leader make.

The online question read:

The President was a guest today on 4 out of the 5 Sunday news shows; the 4 that generally advocate for his Presidency / programs. He did not go on the more critical Fox News. If a goal was to reach out beyond his base, shouldn't Fox News have been included?

Here's my response:

Leadership is predicated on gaining followers. In the case of President Obama, he already has captured all the followers he's going to get via the mainstream media (MSNBC, CNN, the networks). Is that enough to get his legislative agenda passed? Perhaps not, as demonstrated by the awakening of the sleeping giant of conservative—or, at least, not as liberal—citizens across the country participating in Tea Parties and Town Hall meetings.

Americans like a leader who's not afraid, who's willing to take it right to the opposition, who believes enough in his own mind and in the core fairness of the American public to confront the tough questions and defend his policies on the merits. In bypassing Fox News, the President's standing in this regard has taken on some dents. And unnecessarily so. Think of the credibility he would have gained, if only by walking confidently into the alleged "lion's den" of a conservative media television studio.

As a national message development consultant to business leaders, I know that the key obviously is preparation. Figuring out the answers before the questions are asked. Determining the strongest way to make your case with confidence in yourself and command of the material. If CEOs of tech startups and Fortune 200 companies can do this, whether interacting with venture capitalists, shareholders, employees, or customers—all of whom can be as hostile as can be imagined—so should the President of the United States.

We like a President with guts. Preaching to the choir is easy, but cheap. Open-minded citizens want to truly understand what you're advocating, which means taking criticism and taking questions. Many of them watch Fox News. So even at the most basic communications level, come on, Mr. President. Man up.

Discussion Prompts:

1. Do you agree with the statement in the essay that Americans like a President with guts?
2. What benefit can be gained when a leader confronts his or her adversaries directly?
3. What dangers does this tactic present?
4. How would you prepare your leadership client for such a confrontation, from a communications standpoint?

1.15
Poor Sports on Parade

The Big Idea: Like it or not, top athletes are seen and must behave as role models.

They say sports reflect the society in which they flourish. If that's correct, we're in a sorry state these days, if the behavior of two phenomenal superstars this past weekend is any indication.

On Friday evening the NBA inducted Michael Jordan into the Basketball Hall of Fame. No surprise there. The man is a six-time champion, a legend who changed the game with other-worldly moves on the court that retain their jaw-dropping magnificence even after all these years.

Sunday afternoon, Serena Williams competed at the U.S. Open tennis tournament in New York. The power, grace, and dominance she brings to her sport has earned her more Grand Slam titles than any other active female player and more career prize money than any other female athlete in history.

So what's the issue? It's the fact that, even with all of their success, accolades, monetary and personal rewards—or perhaps because of them—both Jordan and Williams let their emotions take over this weekend, embarrassing themselves and their sports by the words they chose.

During his Hall of Fame acceptance speech, Jordan verbally settled scores with individuals and organizations that should have been put to rest years ago. At a critical match point at the U.S. Open, Williams verbally abused a line judge over a disputed call and lost the match as a result.

Longtime NBA star Charles Barkley once famously remarked, "I am not a role model." Oh yeah? Like it or not, famous athletes and celebrities in this society do carry some responsibility to behave appropriately. You want to be famous? That burden comes with the territory, pal, like it or not. Ignore that fact at your own peril.

In my profession, the use of language always has conse-
quences. As a communications consultant to leaders, my advice begins and ends with the assertion that anything my client says or writes becomes part of the permanent record—and
can be resurrected instantly on YouTube or Google. That doesn't
preclude the need to be bold and declarative as needed, but
it does invite a healthy dose of common sense. An ingredient
seemingly in short supply lately.

Boys dribbling basketballs on asphalt courts with chain nets
on the hoops still want to "be like Mike," while girls with sweat-
bands around their heads and swinging racquets with determi-
nation still aspire to Serena's greatness. As individuals reach the
pinnacles of their professions—whether as athletes, performers,
or business leaders—wouldn't it be nice to know that they could
be counted on to use their platforms for positive, constructive,
role-model-worthy communications? As their admirers, fans,
and supporters, we deserve at least that much.

Discussion Prompts:

1. Do you think athletes are role models?
2. What communications counsel would you provide a
    high-profile athlete, in terms of media exposure, social
    media leveraging, public appearances, and so on?
3. How would you advise any of the athletes in this essay
    on how to recover from their mistakes with their fans,
    sponsors, and other interested parties?

Chapter 2
STRATEGY

Somebody has to drive the bus.

There can be a hundred people on the bus, all thinking they know where the bus should go. But until someone gets behind the wheel and makes the bus go there, all you have is a hunk of steel, glass, and rubber packed with inert humanity.

Leaders are the ones who know where the organization needs to go, what it will take to get there, and how to bring others along to contribute to that goal. They're the ones who get to drive the bus. A properly crafted and executed strategy makes the trip easier, smoother, and gives a greater assurance that the group will arrive at its desired destination.

Leadership communications brings a strategy to life. It makes a strategy real, relatable, understandable, tangible, meaningful, and actionable to others throughout an organization. When a leader has identified his or her vision for the group, that vision needs to be translated into words, ideas, and pictures that everyone can grasp and internalize. If the leader is the only one who understands the vision, then how can he or she realistically expect others to contribute toward its achievement?

The "science" of leadership comes in applying a firm understanding of facts, trends, goals, application of available resources, acquisition of needed resources, and countless other considerations. The "art" of leadership, however, entails bringing others along, motivating them through words and actions, instilling a passion fueled by respect and understanding. There can be no other viable means of accomplishing this blending of science and art without clear, consistent, comprehensive communications.

In this chapter, we meet leaders who plunge ahead without having a solid communications strategy in mind, as well as examples of strategic performance that meet the criteria of excellence required of true leaders.

2.1
Jackass in a Hailstorm
The Big Idea: Consistency generates credibility and goodwill for the tough times.

There are moments in the life of a professional communicator when you know the crap is coming. Those are the times that try men's (and women's) souls, not to mention their paychecks and retainer contracts.

The public relations staff at Goldman Sachs knows this, as earnings are about to be released this week, along with announcement of billions in executive bonuses, just a year after accepting massive amounts of federal bailout funds.

How can an organization deal with negative pushback from shareholders, customers, and in this case the taxpaying public in situations like this? Is there any logical, credible, and sustainable defense?

The sunny side is that there indeed is a perfectly good, totally effective, and historically proven way for communicators to help their organizations deal with bad news before it arrives. And it can be summed up in three simple steps:
1. Promote the good.
2. Admit the bad.
3. Explain improvements.

The best bad news is the bad news that you can anticipate. It gives the organization time to think strategically and prepare its messages. By applying all three steps, you can deal with any issue. But by leaving any one of the three out (and you know which one I'm talking about, No. 2) your communications cannot be nearly as effective.

Stonewalling, stalling, or stemwinding verbal feints only give the media and your constituencies reason to keep digging, doubting, and damning. Owning up to shortfalls early—before others define your problems for you—is really the only way to go.

Years ago I worked for a large public utility when the concept of Earth Day was being resurrected for the first time. Coal-burning power plants and a major two-unit nuclear facility didn't exactly endear us to the environmental movement, to say the least, so we knew we were in for some bad press. But it never happened. Here's why.

We made the strategic decision to get way out in front of the Earth Day celebration by becoming completely transparent regarding our environmental record. Truth was we had a very strong story to tell regarding outperforming the toughest federal and state emissions standards, Superfund site cleanups, maintaining water quality, and so on. Not everything was perfect, as might be expected, and we owned up to all of that, as well— along with complete explanations of what we were doing to make things better. We publicized contact names and numbers of key Environmental and Nuclear department leaders, offered to host tours of facilities to media and community groups, and set up a special Earth Day hotline to answer questions and take suggestions from the public about our environmental performance.

The result? Not one story in the media, good or bad, about our company. Not one response to our tour offerings. Not one call to the hotline. Earth Day came and went, and no one gave us a second thought.

Our competitors took another route, clamming up, taking a defensive posture, and getting clobbered with negative stories in the press, protests at their nuclear facilities, and basically taking it on the jaw.

Lesson learned? When bad news is coming, you don't have to just stand there like a jackass in a hailstorm and take it. By promoting the good, admitting the bad, and explaining improvements, you at least take responsibility. And most fair-minded people respect and honor that kind of effort.

Discussion Prompts:

1. Describe a situation in the news where the organization or individual has not "admitted the bad" soon enough or fully enough.
2. How does this shortfall extend the life of the news story?
3. What could have been avoided if the subject had come clean sooner?
4. Why do you think it is so difficult for people to follow this advice?
5. How would you try to address this resistance if you were in charge of communication for the news story subject?

2.2
Steer to the Horizon
The Big Idea: Effective communication is a marathon, not a sprint.

A guy I think the world of told me today he was throwing in the towel. The frustration had reached the tipping point. He'd had enough. A man can only stand so much. No mas, no mas. He'd played his last fantasy football game and was hanging up his pixilated cleats.

To have reached such a definitive conclusion a mere three weeks into this tender young NFL season seemed rather draconian to me and I told him so, but his mind was made up. He'd given it his best shot and had his heart broken. It was over.

How curious we humans can be. We can plan and strategize and hold high hopes for success, but if we take a pie in the face early on, we're ready to give up. The practice of communications in support of business falls victim to this character flaw all too often, I'm sorry to report.

As I work with leaders of organizations—especially those that are just forming, or that are at an early spot on their evolutionary trajectory—a "bet the house" mentality can occur when it comes to message development and delivery. Tight budgets shoulder some of the blame, but it's really more a function of these enthusiastic entrepreneurs simply not having the experience to know that you can't win a war with a single cannon shot, no matter how big.

Simply put, they think—or, perhaps more accurately, they talk themselves into the notion—that issuing a major announcement (once) will get them on the map. That if we make a big enough splash (once), investors and vendors and customers will be beating down their door for the chance to get in on the ground floor of this better mousetrap, whatever it is.

Communications professionals know better. We know human nature. We know that people just aren't that perceptive. Or alert. Or interested. Or smart. You don't win a war with a single cannon blast. It takes lots of cannon, air cover, artillery and infantry. It takes repetition. Establishing the most relevant and persuasive messaging based on careful research and insightful writing, then sending it out to the most appropriate audiences over and over. Consistency and constancy win this race.

As I was learning to drive a car many years ago, the instructor from the driving school would tell me to "steer to the horizon." He said if you drove solely by reacting to road conditions immediately in front of the car, you'd guarantee an accident. It's too stressful, it's too exhausting, and you don't have time to react properly anyway. Instead, he said to look at the road ahead. It's a more reliable and safer way to get where you're going.

All in all, not a bad metaphor for a lot of things in life, including business communications. It's a long road to get people to notice your message, much less understand and act upon it. Keep looking ahead and don't let the potholes along the way slow you down or make you stop. Know where you're going, and why, and how, then steer to the horizon.

Discussion Prompts:

1. A rule of thumb is that a message will not be accepted and retained until it has reached a person seven times. Name at least three ways to simply and cost-effectively keep a client's message going out to the marketplace.
2. Do you think, in the course of sending reinforcing messages to the marketplace, that they should be identical or varied?

2.3
Anybody Can Write, Right?

The Big Idea: Professional writers deserve respect for the service they provide.

In the film "Amadeus," the Emperor of Austria, having enjoyed the public debut of one of Mozart's masterpieces, mulls over what he's just heard and offers this sterling bit of musical insight: "There are too many notes."

Can you imagine? This overstuffed, overpowdered dandy telling the greatest musical genius in history that his composition has "too many notes?" Mozart, nonplussed, bows to the buffoon. His livelihood is on the line, after all. But that doesn't mean he has to listen to such absurd, insulting advice.

The brotherhood and sisterhood of writers has to occasionally deal with lesser lights giving them free advice on their craft, as well. Anyone who thinks he or she can survive as a professional writer without taking a verbal thrashing every now and then is living in Wonderland. If a writer isn't born with a thick skin, he or she had better develop one in a hurry.

Two personal stories illustrate both sides of this particular coin. In the first, we travel back to the summer of 1981 and the newsroom of the late, great Pittsburgh Press newspaper, where I spent 10 weeks as a cub reporter intern on the way toward earning my bachelor's degree in journalism—and where I met Henry.

Henry was a real newspaperman. Think "Lou Grant." He'd covered the big stories, he'd proven his chops hundreds of times over, and now he ran this major metro's city desk. And he didn't suffer substandard work lightly, especially from a carpetbagging bunch of greenhorn college kids like me. As one of my first big assignments, I was sent to cover the discovery of a missing person's corpse one late-June afternoon, and gutlessly danced around the police boundaries, trying to capture just enough information to file the story for the final editions that evening.

After returning to the newsroom and writing the story, I sent it to Henry for proofing. What happened next will be forever seared into my brain. He lit into me in front of 25 other reporters in the open newsroom, loudly peppering me with questions about the story for which I had no answers, challenging me on the structure of the story, screaming that I had completely missed the lead (the opening paragraph that presents the most important information), and generally calling into question my presence in his newsroom.

But then, as my equilibrium slowly began to return and the room stopped spinning, he pointed me back to my desk and sent a message privately to my computer screen, instructing me on who to call for the missing information. Yet I didn't feel insulted. I felt like the greenhorn college kid I was, a novice reporter who had just learned a valuable real-life/real-time lesson unlike anything my professors had ever taught me in a classroom—and one that's remained with me for nearly 30 years.

The second example, however, turned out differently. While working at a company top-heavy with engineers, I was summoned to one such engineer's office to collect comments on a relatively minor article for the employee magazine. After unleashing his red marker all over the draft, he finally looked at me and said, "You know, Tim, I'm an engineer. See those degrees on the wall? I had to really work hard for them. My job takes a lot of intelligence and skill. But, let's face it—anybody can write."

I'm no Mozart, Lord knows, but I knew that I knew more about writing than this guy ever would. So I simply replied, "Are there any factual errors?" When he said that there were not, I stood up, said, "Well then, I'll consider this draft approved," and walked out.

A tough hide comes with the territory. Writers know this. But there's a difference between being asked to accept constructive, respectful criticism and being subjected to cold, offensive insults. I and my fellow writers are professionals too, and deserve to be treated as such. See that degree on the wall?

Discussion Prompts:

1. Have you experienced a dressing-down from an editor or manager regarding your writing yet?
2. How did you react?
3. Are you confident enough to defend your writing?
4. What are your sources of guidance and coaching? If you have none, find one. He or she will help you improve and gain greater confidence in your writing, no matter how long or how briefly you have been practicing the craft.

2.4
Shut Up and Drive, Eldrick
The Big Idea: Self-flagellation can be overdone and backfire.

Okay, so everybody's seen the weird black-and-white, creepy fatherly voiceover, mea culpa, brand-defending commercial starring the world's most famous serial adulterer, Mr. Eldrick Woods. And most people have formed an opinion about it by now, if they care at all.

Here's mine: Shut up and golf already.

Self-styled brand guru Donnie Deutsch gushed on the Today Show last week about what a brave choice Nike made in confronting the issue head-on, and how the 30-second spot did such a courageous, brilliant job in protecting the Nike brand. But honestly, who doesn't know that this guy royally screwed up? (No pun intended.) Who wouldn't agree that his late father would have kicked his rear end had this happened while he was still around? Who could argue that ol' Tiger suffered from a prolonged—and epically so—lapse of judgment?

So we need a sneaker manufacturer to rehash all of this? And not just any sneaker manufacturer, but one that's been swatting away rumors of third-world sweatshop labor practices for years. Pot, meet kettle. What's going on here?

There's a school of thought that believes using Tiger's dad's voice is a skin-crawl-inducing little treat, as well. As we hear Earl Woods scolding his errant son from the Great Beyond, we see the ginned-up shame in poor Tiger's big puppy-dog eyes. Please. We get it. All the emoting, oy! Plus, I've seen better acting at my kids' elementary school Thanksgiving pageants.

Let me play caddy for a moment. Hey, Big Guy, here's the lie on this hole: You're a great golfer but a lousy husband. We're glad you got some help, we're glad you owned up to your colossal and costly collapse of conscience, and we hope things work out for you and your family. It looks like you're learning to control your temper and be more gracious to your fans while on the course, and we're happy about that, too.

But for Pete's sake, can we stop the apology tour yet? You've taken care of the communications requirements by finally telling the truth and expressing remorse. Your most loyal sponsor has piled on with its slightly uncomfortable and off-putting commercial that gently spanks you for being a bad boy before letting you back on the playground with the other kids. Your role model days are on ice for a while, but we shouldn't put you (or any athlete) on that high of a pedestal in the first place, so we'll take the rap on that.

And so, now that everybody's gone to confession and done their penance, there's really only one thing left to say. Tiger, please, just shut up and play.

Discussion Prompts:

1. Do you feel there is such a thing as too much public remorse?
2. Is there a limit to how much patience a celebrity can expect from his or her fan base?
3. Do you think consumers buy products endorsed by celebrities based on the celebrity's professional performance or personal character?
4. How viable and realistic is the practice of expecting public figures to behave like saints in the first place?

2.5
One Reality, Two Truths
The Big Idea: Leaders can manage expectations externally while inspiring internally.

A recent story in the Business section of the *Pittsburgh Post Gazette* offered an overview of a study performed at Penn State University about the effect of "charismatic" language used by CEOs to influence analysts' valuations of companies.

The study concluded that higher levels of charismatic language—defined roughly as inspirational in tone—from CEOs led to slightly more optimistic valuations by analysts. It also noted that allowing charismatic language to shade their estimates of earnings led to less accurate one-year estimates by those analysts.

Lessons learned? For analysts, perhaps be more critical of a CEO's choice of words. For CEOs, weigh your words carefully when addressing external audiences. Truth should be the barometer, as always. But can there be more than one truth?

The truth for a CEO's own employees is that he believes in them. He trusts them to understand, follow, and bring about the organization's vision and goals. He knows they have the enthusiasm, skill, training, and desire to do great things.

The truth for a CEO's shareholders, analysts, regulators, customers, and peers is that the organization has a plan to achieve growth and that he is confident in the resources and people under his leadership to achieve that plan. Not overpromising, nor underestimating. Simply a clear statement of fact and belief.

One reality, two truths. Both truths are accurate while not in conflict. They simply are different expressions of the same belief in the CEO's mind.

Since the study referenced above was conducted at Penn State, it's fitting that the university's legendary head football coach, Joe Paterno, has exemplified this approach in action for decades. During football season, Coach Paterno routinely tamps down expectations of his team and their chances. But he must be much more positive with his players, because Penn State is a perennial powerhouse. One reality, two truths.

Bottom line—it does a CEO little good to pump up the hyperbole when communicating with an external audience, but it does wonders to motivate his own people. If a CEO overstates his case externally when things are going well, observers will be happy to wait for the other shoe to drop and he's brought low once more. If he does it when things are going poorly, his credibility will be shot from the start. Yet within his organization, employees look to the CEO to provide a steady vision and a heartfelt endorsement of confidence and pride.

To truly lead, CEOs should use language to energize internally and set more prudent expectations externally. One reality, two truths.

Discussion Prompts:

1. Do you agree with the premise of this essay?
2. Why or why not?
3. Can internal cheerleading do more harm than good?
4. How? Under what circumstances?

2.6

'Mr. Hayes, have you ever had to lie?'

The Big Idea: Public relations' role is to advance the organization, not to do the job of journalists.

One of my favorite perks as a middle-aged professional comes in visiting college classes as a guest speaker. Inevitably, standing before a class of young aspiring communicators, I know two questions will be coming my way: "How much do you make?" and "Have you ever had to lie?"

The first one's easy—"That's none of your business." But the second takes a little more explanation and context. The short answer is "No," which typically generates skeptical glances from the assembled journalism and PR majors, so I dive into the real world applications of how information gets generated, distributed, and processed between business and the media.

My good fortune put me in a small-market newspaper newsroom right out of college, a newly minted B.A. in journalism in my hand. As a cub reporter in the early 1980s, my daily mission was to find and write about both sides of every story, just as my professors drilled into my thick head as a student. Media's role rested on its responsibility to remain objective, critical, balanced, fair. And that meant gathering information from every perspective related to a story, sifting through it, and presenting a comprehensive picture to the reader.

In time, I left the newsroom and entered the field of public relations, where the role changed into presenting my organization's side of the story as accurately, powerfully, and persuasively as possible. My job no longer carried the charge of being balanced. Instead, it meant promoting the philosophy, practices, personalities, products, and perspective of my employer to the media.

It was up to those in the media to take the information I now made available to them, find an opposing or alternate viewpoint, and present a picture that balanced the two, in other words.

Back to the college classroom question of being pressured to lie in the course of performing my PR duties, the answer again has always been no. Does that mean that I and my various colleagues along the way have been selective in how our messages have been fashioned for release to the media? Absolutely. If you would label those "sins of omission," so be it. Have we gone out of our way to list opposing opinions or help the media find those who would disagree with our organization's point of view? Hell no—that's their job.

In a publicly traded business, providing a return to shareholders is the number one responsibility, period. A successful business does that by producing a product or service that meets an identified need better than its competitors. Public relations supports that effort by protecting and promoting the business, thereby building goodwill and trust among its employees and customers. Outright lying would destroy that trust, as has been proven time and again over the years.

I can sleep at night knowing that anything I've ever written for an employer or client has been accurate and truthful in its own right—and would assert that 99 percent of my fellow professional communicators could say the same. And when I share that with the kids in college, they know it's the truth.

Discussion Prompts:

1. **What do you think of this essay's main point—that communications must serve the truth while also serving the organization's objectives?**
2. **What do you think would be the challenges in successfully bridging those two responsibilities at all times?**

3. Describe an instance of an organization that lost its credibility and value in the marketplace by intentionally misleading people.

2.7
Change the Questions!
The Big Idea: Professionals keep their cool during crises.

It was one of those times when every member of an in-house public relations staff had to really be on his or her game. The company had made some bad mistakes, investors began getting restless, regulators smelled blood, and the media wasn't about to let up.

My role in coping with this particular house afire was to develop a series of media questions-and-answers for executives to use during press conferences and telephone interviews with reporters—a standard tool meant to limit any ad-libbing under pressure and to ensure a consistency of message emanating from the company.

The Q&As developed for the executive team pulled no punches. Every potential "gotcha" question made it to the document, along with verifiable and forthright responses. Having been a reporter earlier in my career, I wanted our guys to be ready for anything the media could throw at them. They were in for some uncomfortable give-and-take with the press, so realistic preparation remained paramount and prudent.

We sent the materials upstairs for review, and what came back to me from the chief financial officer still blows my mind. He had slashed in angry red marker across the entire first page: **CHANGE THE QUESTIONS!**

My first reaction? Stunned silence. My second? Nervous laughter quickly spinning into raucous guffaws that drew the attention of my compatriots in the Corporate Communications Department. My third? An icy numbness down the center of my cerebellum as I realized the CFO wasn't kidding.

So instead of manning up and properly preparing for the media firestorm minutes away, he decided that adopting an alternate reality where nobody asked unpleasant questions about touchy subjects made for a better, smarter, more winning strategy. Ridiculous didn't begin to describe the situation.

Since the Q&A was my responsibility, it fell to me to go into his office and explain that we couldn't actually tell the reporters to rephrase their questions, no matter how prickly or unnerving they may sound to us. But before I did that, I reworked the Q&A document just enough that the questions covered the same topics and led to the same answers. The CFO felt better, the answers remained consistent, and no one was the wiser.

The moral of this story? Good preparation always will help an organization deal with crises, even if you have to assuage egos a little along the way. This particular executive dealt with his blossoming, ripening anxiety by making a ludicrous demand. By altering the "means" and humoring him a tad, the organization reached its desired "end"—a successful series of media interviews that kept our message clear, credible, and consistent.

Discussion Prompts:
Even executives can crack under high pressure situations, but that's where communications experts need to perform their duties at even higher levels of consistency and excellence. Can you think of another way to have handled this CFO's unusual request, while still achieving the larger organizational goal of ensuring consistency of message?

Chapter 3
MESSAGING

Portraying the Almighty in the movie, "Oh, God!," George Burns laments to his modern day Moses, John Denver, about the human race, "You've figured out so many ways to communicate with each other, that finally no one can."

In the world of leadership communication, even people who seemingly speak the same language can't always connect with each other properly or well.

It may be a function of *perspective*—where the leader's view of an organization's issues or problems is by necessity different from those of the frontline people further down on the chart.

It may be function of *understanding*—where the leader simply knows so much more (or less) about an issue or problem, that employees have trouble relating to the messages being sent.

Or it may be function of *trust*—where the leader has been lacking in providing regular communications, so a sense of doubt and skepticism has been permitted to build among the employee base.

There are a thousand reasons why communication either works or doesn't work, and the form that the message takes fulfills a critical function in the process. One of the cardinal rules of public relations is to take the time to understand your audience before you begin formulating your communications. That's unfortunately the point from which most failures to communicate emanate.

Leaders need followers. The best way to enlist and engage those followers is to envelop them in messages that speak to their unique perspectives, their levels of understanding, and in an environment of trust—as built on a consistent, persistent, insistent platform of ongoing outreach.

The essays in this chapter touch on stories where leaders carried out this responsibility well, or not so well. Regardless, the importance of quality messaging as a means of strengthening the capabilities of true leaders comes through in each instance.

3.1
Tale of Two Blown Calls
The Big Idea: It's not always about you.

Bad stuff happens. Some of it's foreseeable, but most of the lousy breaks come at us unannounced, and before you know it the boat's been swamped and you're flailing in the water looking for dry land.

The BP oil rig explosion in the Gulf of Mexico caught the giant corporation off guard, and it's been nearly two months with no clear end in sight to the gusher that's despoiling aquatic life and soon much of the U.S. southern coastlands.

Having worked at companies that create environmental impacts, I believe BP when it says the last thing they wanted was to have this disaster happen—and that they are trying everything they can to stop it and clean it up. Huge companies like that do care about their impact on the environment because it's important to their ability to remain in business, to generate profits for their shareholders, to provide ongoing employment to their people, to pay taxes to local, state, and federal governments, and to supply products to their customers. It has become sadly apparent, though, that BP has been plagued by good intentions and poor execution.

That's why the messages being crafted and delivered by BP leaders has become so vital. With each day the deep sea oil continues to pollute the Gulf, BP's credibility becomes more strained. If the company has any hope of holding on to its investors and its customers, we need to have some shred of faith in what it says—because we're rapidly losing faith in what it does.

So when BP's CEO Tony Hayward said on NBC last Sunday, as he began to offer an apology to residents of the Gulf region, "There's no one who wants this thing over more than I do...I'd like my life back."—the firestorm erupted. Talk about the exact wrong message. There has been loss of life, millions of gallons of crude oil washing up on previously pristine and highly valued resort destinations, promises and pledges and a deepening sense of disappointment and disaster. And the CEO just wants his life back?

Hayward has since apologized, acknowledging the insensitivity and insulting tone of his verbal slip-up. But the truest qualities of people come out most when the heat is on. We may have gotten a glimpse into the heart of BP's top man the other day, and it's not the most reassuring view.

On the other hand, we saw the heart of another man who made a monumental mistake this week, but who shouldered the blame, expressed sincere remorse, and offered an example of accountability, fortitude, and gratitude for the forgiveness he received. Major League Baseball umpire Jim Joyce called a runner safe at first base when he clearly was out on the replay. That doesn't sound so bad until you realize that the play would have been the final out of a perfect game as pitched by Detroit Tiger pitcher Armondo Galarraga—only the 21st perfect game in baseball history.

Joyce was inconsolable after the game, realizing what his blown call meant to the pitcher and to baseball in general. He said, "I missed it, I missed it...I took a perfect game away from that kid over there who worked his ass off all night...This wasn't just any call, this was a history call, and I kicked the s*** out of it...If I had been Galarraga I would have been the first one out there, but he didn't say a word, not a word."

Joyce still felt bad at the next night's game, when he was assigned to umpire at home plate. In a classy moment, Galarraga brought the team's starting lineup card out to the teary-eyed Joyce at home plate and shook his hand, showing there were no hard feelings.

Grace or selfishness? Class or self-pity? Don't tell me that messages delivered during bad moments don't matter or can't be helped. The severity of the two instances couldn't be farther apart, of course. But if adversity brings out character, we saw two terrific examples this week.

Discussion Prompts:

1. Should leaders be allowed to express their personal feelings during a crisis?
2. What are the potential positive and negative ramifications of doing so?
3. Where would you draw the line between a CEO's responsibility to represent the organization, and his or her justification in speaking from a more personal perspective? Why?

3.2
The Perfect American Speech
The Big Idea: Great oratory stands on noble concepts expressed magnificently.

On this Independence Day, I'm thinking of the incredibly powerful and elegant words of the Declaration of Independence, naturally. But I'm also thinking of a document that I believe completed and elevated the thoughts of the Declaration as well as the Constitution—Lincoln's Gettysburg Address. To my mind, the perfect American speech.

Only two minutes in length, and delivered on November 19, 1863, four months after the monumental battle had been fought, President Abraham Lincoln crystallized for eternity the essence of all things American. Stripped down to its essence for a modern audience, here are Lincoln's main points:

This nation began with high ideals—perhaps too high—and we're at war to see if those ideals can survive. A tremendous number of men died on this land over those ideals, and it's up to us to make sure that sacrifice wasn't wasted. If we can do that, this nation is sure to pass this greatest of tests.

That's the TV Guide summary version, but how much more beautifully those thoughts were phrased by this lanky lawyer, this frustrated writer, this bearded genius in a stovepipe hat. "...We cannot dedicate, we cannot consecrate, we cannot hallow this ground..." "...From these honored dead we take increased devotion to that cause for which they gave the last full measure of devotion..." "...That this nation, under God, shall have a new birth of freedom..." "...That government of the people, by the people, for the people shall not perish from the earth..."

It is said that the Founding Fathers' bold proclamation in the Declaration of Independence, "We hold these truths to be self-evident that all men are created equal," carried a shadow cast by the taint of slavery. Four score and seven years later, Abraham Lincoln, the Great Emancipator, made his own bold proclamation at Gettysburg of "a new birth of freedom," framing the War Between the States as the fight for freedom for all Americans and completing the noble cause begun by Jefferson, Adams, Hamilton, Washington, and all who fought for independence.

Lincoln was preceded at the podium during the cemetery dedication ceremony by Edward Everett, a noted orator of the day. Everett spoke for two punishing hours; the President for two immortal minutes. Everett told Lincoln later, "My speech will soon be forgotten; yours never will be. How gladly I would exchange my hundred pages for your twenty lines."

Indeed, of the entire Gettysburg Address, I can only find one phrase that does not ring true or inspiring. Lincoln said, "The world will little note nor long remember what we say here..." How wrong he was. For in encapsulating the true and fulfilled spirit of this nation—one with liberty and justice for all, regardless of race or religion or any other quantifier—Lincoln's masterpiece of speechwriting became the perfect American speech.

Discussion Prompts:

1. Think of examples where a lot of information is delivered in a very short period of time. What makes those examples effective?
2. What makes them lacking in effectiveness?
3. Take position either for or against texting and Tweeting as message delivery vehicles and hold a debate with others in your group.

3.3
Your Baby Is Ugly
The Big Idea: Understand your audience and keep it simple.

There's an episode of "Seinfeld" where Jerry, Elaine and the gang head to the Hamptons to stay with some friends because they "gotta see the baby." The problem, though, is that the poor little thing is the ugliest infant they've ever seen, but they obviously can't say that to the parents. The closest anybody gets to uttering the truth is a visiting pediatrician, who calls the infant "breathtaking."

As a professional communications consultant to entrepreneurial leaders, sometimes I've had to tell people their "baby"—even while deploying "breathtaking" technology or other features—is nonetheless ugly. Or, at the very least, so mired in jargon and indecipherable, extraneous, irrelevant detail that no one can figure out why their company exists, what their product does, and most important, why anybody should care about or be willing to pay for it.

Achieving simplicity of message can be really complicated. In business, especially among brilliant minds from the university or research community, the hardest part I've found comes in convincing them that no one cares what their logo means, or the intricacies of the interior code built into the software, or that their two vice presidents scored major fellowships.

I spent three hours one interminable afternoon in a coffee shop listening to a pair of very bright entrepreneurs tell me everything—and I mean every single thing—about their new web-based application for franchise operators. Normally a decaf drinker, I kept loading up on the highest-octane brew that barista could muster, just to remain focused and attentive. A full 180 minutes later, I had to ask them to please stop educating me because I needed to get to another client appointment.

In government, the worst offender every year in the ugly baby contest is the annual State of the Union address to Congress. The President, in fulfilling this Constitutionally mandated update, typically gets more help than is actually helpful as every federal department and agency competes to get a paragraph or more in the speech. In the end, more often than not, we are treated to a dog's breakfast of unconnected wishes, chest-beating claims, and manufactured applause lines.

Say, here's an idea. Whether in business, politics, entertainment, education, or any other field of endeavor—let's take our lead from the noble carpenter who advises us to measure twice and cut once. When communicating, let's think longer and write shorter. Let's whittle ideas down to a shiny sheen of clarity and relevance. I'd bet the farm we'd get more done in less time, because people would know just what the heck is going on and why the heck it's so important to them. For once.

A fellow I once worked for thought if a proposal passed what he called the "plop test"—meaning the document was hefty enough to make a loud *plop!* when you dropped it on a desk—that made it a good proposal. Every time he said that, the professional writer inside me cringed. Plop test? More like flop test, if you ask me. Entrepreneurs do make some genuinely breathtaking "babies." For heaven's sake, let's stop uglying them up.

Discussion Prompts:

1. This essay calls on entrepreneurs and communicators to "think longer and write shorter." Do you agree, and why or why not?
2. When would it be advantageous to get into the minutiae of a new technology in a communications exercise?
3. How do you think a reporter would prefer to learn about a new technology?

3.4
Chicken Little as Speechwriter?
The Big Idea: When everything is important, nothing is.

An old boss once said to me, "The hardest thing in the world to change is someone's mind." And, as a professional communicator and speechwriter, I've come to see the wisdom in that notion.

In business, communications plays to both sides of the human brain. You line up your facts into a logical sequence and tell a story to humanize them, so that your ideas are both understood and embraced.

Then there's the world of politics, where the likelihood of changing minds may be small, but the chance to make the other side abandon parts of their plans based on pressure, embarrassment, or pragmatism is much higher. It's a game I never enjoyed playing, but it sure is fascinating to watch.

As an observer of political rhetoric, I see a risky but regretfully successful speechwriting strategy being used in the current healthcare reform debate. This strategy first uses inflated, overblown language to describe the opposition's stance. That mischaracterization, then, becomes the dominant focus of the next few news cycles, leading to the real end game—to swing the pendulum of public awareness, debate, and negative pressure so far to one side that the opposition's original stance is either watered-down or abandoned altogether.

The recent statement by former Alaska Gov. Sarah Palin, that the healthcare bill in Congress called for "death panels" of federal bureaucrats deciding whether elderly and ailing Americans would receive healthcare, I believe falls into this category. Palin based her statement on a section of the bill referencing end-of-life consultations. Taxpayer fears about government intervention and control of healthcare fed into this incendiary phrase, which catapulted to the headlines of newspapers and cable news shows for days.

The growing firestorm led to the removal of all end-of-life provisions in a version bill being considered in the U.S. Senate, which I'm guessing was the ultimate goal of Palin and her supporters all along. The House bill still has some end-of-life provisions, but a final bill will need to be hammered out in conference so any remaining provisions may be removed or modified as well.

Make no mistake, I don't mean to point fingers at Palin alone. Quite the contrary. This approach gets put into action by both sides of the political aisle constantly, regardless of whoever's in power or whatever's the issue. So there's little disputing that this sort of "Chicken Little" communications strategy works in the political realm, where changing minds takes a backseat to roundhouse punches to the loyal opposition.

But as a professional communicator and someone who respects the integrity of language and the leaders entrusted to use it, that sort of thing nevertheless turns my stomach. After all, for Pete's sake, whether you're Republican or Democrat, conservative or liberal, right or left wing, the sky isn't *always* falling.

Discussion Prompts:

1. A key rule of communications is to understand your audience. When your audience is the entire voting population, can the message ever be lofty or inspiring?
2. Or does the "lowest common denominator" mean political speech must be kept to the widest generalities possible?
3. How would either choice affect a candidate's ability to govern once elected?

3.5

Don'tcha Just Love a Good Story?

The Big Idea: To influence behavior, couch your message in a relatable story.

At a lunchtime gathering of speechwriters I attended last week in New York City, longtime political and business speechwriter Robert Lehrman shared some of the more potent and important lessons he's learned along the way, and one hit me with a special resonance. He said, in describing what made the better speeches of his legendary career indeed better, "Evidence alone is not enough. It takes persuasive storytelling."

Mr. Lehrman closed his comments to the roomful of speechwriting peers with another gem that I've stored in my memory bank and share with you here. He said, "Opening a speech with a story is the best way to help an audience with retaining the messages to follow—plus, people like it best when you open with a story."

In a recent Newsweek profile of Al Gore and a new book he's written, we find the following passage:

"To anyone with bad memories of how Gore's fact-filled debate performances against George W. Bush in 2000 failed to connect with voters, it may come as no surprise that Our Choice has a graphic on 'how a wind turbine works,'...But because of one sentence, and one chapter, it does surprise. The chapter is an astute analysis of the psychological barriers that keep most Americans from taking the threat of climate change seriously, his acknowledgment that emotion, not just reason, drives the decisions people make. The sentence is this: 'Simply laying out the facts won't work.'"

This shared perspective on the importance of appealing to emotion makes it no surprise that Mr. Lehrman served as a lead speechwriter for Mr. Gore in the Clinton Administration.

As a professional communications consultant, I know that my clients' credibility and credence rest on a bedrock of verifiable and thoroughly vetted facts. As a professional speechwriter, I also know that my clients' duty to their audience is to convey those facts within the context of relatable stories.

A speech is not a research paper standing on its hind legs. A speech must be a performance, a story, with a beginning, middle and end. The audience has no idea what's coming. It's all new to them. Spewing a recitation of cold facts and numbers at an audience goes beyond poor speechgiving—it's unfair and disrespectful.

Organizations invite speakers because they have some level of expectation from that person regarding subject matter, expertise, insight, and revelation. Sure, facts and supporting data build the skeleton of the speech, but is that all there is? Think how uninteresting and indistinct the world would be if all you could see of anyone else was their skeleton.

No, it's the flesh and blood that make people fascinating and different. In the same way, the flesh and blood of human experience and relatable stories that wrap around the factual skeleton of a speech give it life, make it memorable, and spur audiences to act. Because in the end, nobody likes a lecture, but everybody loves a good story.

Discussion Prompts:

1. President Reagan began the practice of spotlighting someone in the gallery during the State of the Union Address—a device still used today. What does this technique accomplish for the President?
2. Why has each succeeding President continued this tradition, especially during that particular speech?
3. Pick an issue important to you, list the facts supporting your position, then look for a story to illustrate at least one of the key points. Evaluate the impact of conveying information in this manner.

❖ ❖ ❖

3.6

A Great Ending is Only the Beginning

The Big Idea: An audience deserves an energetic, thought-provoking conclusion.

All right, show of hands, please: How many of you knew that, in the original script for the first "Rocky" movie written by Sylvester Stallone, Rocky dies after the climactic fight that ends the film?

Thank goodness wiser heads prevailed. Not only would that have been the ultimate downer, but I would wager that "Rocky" would never have won the Academy Award for Best Picture if that original ending had remained.

For those of you old enough to remember, "Rocky" was a phenomenon in 1977 because it featured a true hero with positive values who worked hard to overcome long odds, and who—even though he didn't win the boxing match—won something more, the love of a woman and validation of his own self-worth. In the mid-1970s, a story of courage, perseverance, and ultimate triumph was not corny or hackneyed—it was revolutionary, and it caught lightning in a bottle. And for my money, it all came down to that wonderful, chaotic, uplifting ending of the film.

A great ending sticks with an audience, whether they're in a movie theater sharing a cinematic experience or in an auditorium listening to a speaker. A great ending spurs people to action.

The first time I saw "Rocky," I was sixteen years old and was so inspired that I literally ran the mile and a half home from the theater—something I had never done before and have never done since. But that explosive ending did something to me, to my brain, to my adrenal glands, and it ended up in my legs and my Converse All-Star sneakers as I sprinted like a teenager possessed, up and down hills, streets, and alleys all the way to my back door, breathless, wild-eyed, ready to take on the world.

A great ending can lift a speaker's audience too. Think of Martin Luther King Jr.'s stemwinder at the conclusion of his "I Have a Dream" speech:

"When we allow freedom to ring, when we let it ring from every village and every hamlet, from every state and every city, we will be able to speed up that day when all of God's children, black men and white men, Jews and Gentiles, Protestants and Catholics, will be able to join hands and sing in the words of the old Negro spiritual, 'Free at last! Free at last! Thank God Almighty, we are free at last!'"

Chills. Nearly fifty years later.

The speech doesn't have to be one for the ages, though. A strong ending works no matter what the venue or the context. I wrote a commencement speech for an executive that ended with the following:

"Penn State has prepared you, even amid all the uncertainty in the world today. Plus, the Penn State alumni network is the largest in the world—you're joining an amazing global force today. With that in mind, here's your final pop quiz as a student here: **WE—ARE!**" The graduates then enthusiastically shouted back, **"PENN—STATE!"** My speaker wrapped things up quickly by saying, **"**You all pass with flying colors. Blue and white, of course." The entire gathering felt tremendous positive energy for themselves, their school, and their commencement speaker, all stemming from a great ending.

Too often, speakers and speechwriters stumble, trip, even crawl across the finish line with limp statements that convey relief it's over. Don't do that. Sprint across that finish line! Get your audience juiced up and keep them there all the way to the end. Challenge them, surprise them, inspire them, give them something to act upon. Give them a great ending that keeps you and your message top of mind.

Who knows? They might even want to run the whole way home.

Discussion Prompts:

1. Some say a speech is nothing more than: tell then what you're going to tell them, tell them, and tell them what you just told them. Would you want to sit through something so lifeless?

2. Write a three-paragraph ending to a speech about your career to date, writing it in a way that would capture an audience's attention to the very end.

3.7
Politics as Primer
The Big Idea: Political rhetoric can influence the language of all leaders.

Politics, it seems, never leaves the national consciousness. As the mid-term Congressional election season begins to get in gear, we can learn much—regardless of personal party affiliation or policy stances—about the power of persuasive language.

Whether dealing with a business topic, a political cause or a personal message, the same elements apply. A speech is not a glorified research paper, or at least it shouldn't be. Instead, a speech should present relevant information cloaked in an entertaining and engaging manner, designed so that those hearing it remember key ideas. A great speech also envelops those ideas in classic turns of phrase, like these:

"This nation is a shining city on a hill."—*President Ronald Reagan*

"We will not tire, we will not falter, and we will not fail. Freedom and fear, justice and cruelty, have always been at war, and we know that God is not neutral between them. "- President George W. Bush

"If the British Empire and its Commonwealth last for a thousand years, men will still say, 'This was their finest hour.'"—*British Prime Minister Winston Churchill*

"The energy, the faith, the devotion which we bring to this endeavor will light our country and all who serve it—and the glow from that fire can truly light the world."—*President John F. Kennedy*

"I have a dream that my four little children will one day live in a nation where they will not be judged by the color of their skin, but by the content of their character."—*Martin Luther King, Jr.*

"That government of the people, by the people, for the people shall not perish from the earth."—President Abraham Lincoln

These words endure—some more than 140 years since they were uttered. And why? Because they not only transmitted information, they stirred emotions, they excited souls. The listeners' brains may have recorded the words, but the listeners' hearts registered the moment. And therein lies all the difference.

Americans hear much political rhetoric, some soaring, some sophomoric. But those individuals who must speak publicly, whether leading a business or a movement, can glean valuable insights from the world of politics as to what makes the spoken word the most powerful form of human expression—insights that effectively empower leaders of any stripe.

From where will the next great leaders emerge? When? And will such leaders maximize the tremendous force for positive change that persuasive language creates? If they hope to be great, they must.

Discussion Prompts:
1. What is your favorite political phrase or saying?
2. What makes that statement meaningful and memorable for you?
3. Can a leader emerge without having good oratorical skills?
4. How important is the message, if the speaker is very good using oratory?
5. Why or why not?

3.8
Rising Above the Spam-alanche

The Big Idea: It takes careful thought to stand out among communications clutter.

The first time it happened, I quickly moved the cursor around, selected "Add Sender to Blocked Sender List," clicked the mouse and thought it was all over with.

As my kids would say: "Fail."

That happened years ago and since then at least 50 e-mails a day arrive, offering discounted rates on male-specific pharmaceuticals, beautiful replica watches, online college degrees, and even available Russian brides who remind me of "the wonderful memories we created in Moscow last year."

Huh?!

The deluge of unwanted, unread, unnecessary, unbelievable, unappreciated messages would be funny if it weren't such a nuisance—and such a colossal waste of time. Honestly, does anyone—anyone—actually respond to this nonsense? Anyone who does deserves whatever they get, whether it's a financial rip-off, a stolen identity, or anything in between. They sure as heck aren't getting a Russian bride showing up on their doorstep courtesy of the FedEx guy.

It's one of life's true mysteries. When I get the exact same bothersome e-mail 10 times a day for three months straight—with the only difference being the sender's e-mail address—I wonder who's behind this? What do they hope to accomplish? How do they find the time for this crap? And what makes this form of electronic harassment such fun for them?

As a professional communications consultant to leaders, I know that repeating a message helps an audience retain it, but this is ridiculous!

I've seen studies that conclude Americans get assaulted by 3,000 messages a day on average. Not all come through the computer or telephone, but also from TV, radio, billboards, newspapers, magazines, and on and on.

When so many of them are completely silly, stupid, hopeless, and hapless, how in the world can vital, vibrant, relevant, meaningful, positive, constructive, worthwhile, valuable messages hope to stand out and get noticed? The answer is both alarmingly simple and frighteningly difficult to achieve:

<u>Think harder.</u>

Know both what you want to communicate and what your most important audience needs to hear. That alone represents an enormous level of effort and understanding. Then, armed with that knowledge, craft your message to attract your audience's attention and present the information in a fresh way. Lots of thought required there, as well.

The bad news? As British philosopher and social critic Bertrand Russell said, "Most people would rather die than think; in fact, they do so." On the other hand, those who do think, succeed—whether in leadership communications or in any other walk of life.

Sorry, I must be going now. Need to deal with a fresh load of unordered spam.

Discussion Prompts:

Imagine you are responsible for getting publicity for your client at a major community event that has multiple sponsors. List three ideas to attract attention without spending anything on paid advertising or sponsorships.

3.9
Playing for Keeps with Mind Games
The Big Idea: People evaluate intellectually but act emotionally.

"The most basic state of mind that leaders need to understand is the will of their constituencies: their will to work, their will to live, their will to revolt, their will to follow you."

So says Jim Clifton, Chairman and CEO of Gallup, in a recent interview in the Gallup Management Journal. His main point for today's leaders comes down to a basic premise—that Six Sigma, lean manufacturing, process improvements, quality circles, and the rest of the inwardly focused production efficiency tools have pretty much been internalized. They have been perfected and are now expected. They are not differentiators any longer—they are the price of admission to the competitive ballgame.

Instead, Clifton says that true leaders in the marketplace of 2010 and beyond must recognize and act upon two new premises—that human decision-making is more emotional than rational, and that leaders must understand the minds of their employees, customers, regulators, and investors. The ones who do can use that knowledge to create real economic growth, more new jobs, and emerge as true differentiated organizations.

Based on these insightful observations, I see leadership communications playing a pivotal role. Story telling, relating the organization's macro vision to the audience's micro viewpoint, will be a key component in appealing to the mind of a leader's constituencies. Perhaps put in a more pedestrian and cynical statement, everything needs to come down to the baseline question asked by employees, customers, and other groups: "What's in it for me?" Or, phrased in a more positive light, leaders must answer their constituencies' request: "Help me to care."

In employee training modules I've written for a service industry, for example, every lesson centered around personal behaviors, along with an explanation of how and why those behaviors benefit both employee and customer. These were not designed as dry lectures, but as interactive stories where the employees being trained could feel and experience the effects of on-the-job behaviors—and thereby not only retain the information mentally, but apply those lessons emotionally on a practical basis with their real-life customers. Customer satisfaction ratings have been on a steady upward track ever since.

Some years ago I worked in support of a non-profit hospital foundation. All outreach communications to active and potential donors centered on two ideas—first, how the donor personally benefits from making a gift (through building up lives of people in less-fortunate situations), and second, by telling stories of specific outcomes achieved on behalf of children, the infirmed, and families through such donations. We never talked about the foundation itself—only about how the lives of donors and recipients got happier and healthier. Within three years, donations went up more than 200 percent.

In the end, it's the performance of people that make the real difference. But clear communication of a leader's vision—acting on Clifton's observation that understanding the minds of constituencies is the only way to differentiate today—is essential in helping that performance come to its fullest fruition.

Discussion Prompts:

When people see why they should care, they usually do. Describe a personal example of becoming involved or engaged in a cause or activity after learning why and how it affected your life.

3.10
Medaling in the Winter Rhetoricalympics
The Big Idea: Inspiring communications can come in many forms.

In the spirit of the Vancouver games now under way, today we inaugurate the Winter Rhetoricalympics, a recognition of notable, surprising, or inspiring statements that occur within the timeframe of the real Olympics but that do not necessarily have anything to do with the Olympics. Okay, got it? Here we go...

In third place, taking the Rhetoricalympics Bronze, is famed movie critic Roger Ebert, who has lost his jaw, his ability to eat or drink, and his ability to speak after several surgical procedures to combat thyroid cancer. In a wonderful, touching piece in *Esquire* magazine, Ebert at one point scribbles on a Post-It Note— the only way he can communicate, and a method he uses to the hilt—these words:

"There is no need to pity me. Look how happy I am. This has led to an exploring of writing."

Having become famous through the TV show "At the Movies" with his friend, the late Gene Siskel, people forget or never knew that Ebert is first and foremost a fantastic writer. He still reviews movies and one visit to his website at www.rogerebert.com proves that he's not lost a step.

Yet his life has changed so drastically that it's truly an inspiration to know that Roger Ebert's joy in living and in writing remains so strong.

Earning the Rhetoricalympics Silver is Kutilda Woods, Tiger's mother. During the 13 minutes of confession and apology that the world's most famous and infamous golfer shared this week, it became impossible to not notice the conflicting combination of shame, embarrassment, love, and pride that perhaps only a mother can bear.

Mrs. Woods at times could not bring herself to look at her son directly as he tried to place the first brick in the long process of repairing his family, rebuilding his reputation, and restoring his career. At other points, her gaze was so intense at Tiger, almost willing him on silently from her front-row seat. She was the first person he went to after the remarks were finished, and her comments to the media after the event had a strong flavor of maternal defiance and protection.

Say what you will about Tiger, but you can't fault his mom.

And the top prize in this edition of the Rhetoricalympics, taking the Gold, is U.S. Sen. Evan Bayh, a politician who had the guts to say what millions of Americans think—that our current crop of leaders in Washington, on both sides of the aisle, deserve to be broomed out of office this November. On Feb. 16, it was reported on Yahoo News that:

Newly retiring Sen. Evan Bayh declared the American political system "dysfunctional," riddled with "brain-dead partisanship" and permanent campaigning. Flatly denying any possibility that he'd seek the presidency or any other higher office, Bayh argued that the American people needed to deliver a "shock" to Congress by voting incumbents out en masse and replacing them with people interested in reforming the process and governing for the good of the people, rather than deep-pocketed special-interest groups.

In the days that followed, political observers opined on what pushed Bayh to express such taboo ideas. Maybe it's just a matter of someone finally deciding to speak the truth in Washington, DC? Now, this blog is not meant to be a stage for political debate, and I am not taking sides here. I just believe that anyone with the gumption and the guts to so boldly break through the stifling political chatter deserves some recognition.

Discussion Prompts:

1. Every now and then, someone in politics actually tells the unvarnished truth. Describe an issue within your universe where a round of straight truth-telling could do some good.
2. What needs to be said?
3. Who would be the best person to say it?
4. What would happen next?

3.11
A $40 Million Piece of Writing
The Big Idea: A well-crafted letter can achieve amazing things.

Speechwriters, political pundits, and columnists have been hard at work combing over such recent high-profile events as President Obama's State of the Union address, the acceptance remarks made by Senator-elect Scott Brown of Massachusetts, and even Robert Downey Jr.'s sarcastic quips at the Golden Globes.

But I've been more interested in another piece of writing that may have had a more immediate impact on a lot more people—namely, Conan O'Brien's statement rejecting NBC's proposal to move his "Tonight Show" to after midnight to make room for a 30-minute show featuring Jay Leno.

When you stop and read this letter, it truly is a well-crafted statement of pride, defiance, and guts, with a healthy dose of thumb-in-the-eye, pie-in-the-face, good-guy vs. bad-guy, show-biz humor and spunk. Here's what I mean.

First, O'Brien frames the issue in its proper perspective: *"In the last few days, I've been getting a lot of sympathy calls, and I want to start by making it clear that no one should waste a second feeling sorry for me. For 17 years, I've been getting paid to do what I love most and, in a world with real problems, I've been absurdly lucky."*

He then moves into a chronological recitation of facts leading up to the source of the conflict, NBC's need to unfairly scapegoat his show for the network's overall poor ratings: *"After only seven months, with my Tonight Show in its infancy, NBC has decided to react to their terrible difficulties in prime-time by making a change in their long-established late night schedule."*

Next, O'Brien defends the history and legacy of the Tonight Show against the network's untenable short-term solution: *"I sincerely believe that delaying the Tonight Show into the next day* to accommodate another comedy program will seriously damage what I consider to be the greatest franchise in the history of broadcasting. The Tonight Show at 12:05 simply isn't the Tonight Show. Also, if I accept this move I will be knocking the Late Night show, which I inherited from David Letterman and passed on to Jimmy Fallon, out of its long-held time slot. That would hurt the other NBC franchise that I love, and it would be unfair to Jimmy."

And lastly he fires a parting shot to solidify the villain in this skirmish and to express pride in his team's performance, even though he acknowledges that their ship will sink: "My hope is that NBC and I can resolve this quickly so that my staff, crew, and I can do a show we can be proud of, for a company that values our work."

So from an opening couched in humility to a clear depiction of who's to blame, and from a bold denunciation of an unacceptable proposal to a proud defense of his production's record, O'Brien's statement to the network stands as a solidly crafted, well-reasoned piece of writing. And even though he lost his show and went through a very public embarrassment, a $40 million-plus check to just go away ain't all bad.

Just goes to show what a well-written letter can accomplish.

Discussion Prompts:
Write a mock letter to a senior manager defending your department's program against threatened severe budget cuts affecting staff, equipment, and support. The letter cannot exceed 500 words.

3.12
Nobody Gets to See the Great Oz!
The Big Idea: Leaders living in cocoons risk losing the respect of those they lead.

We were going for our first mortgage many years ago, when our bank called and asked to see yet another set of documents. I took them to work with me the next day and left the office building mid-morning to walk the three blocks or so to meet with the banker.

At that point in time, we lived in a town where the central business district was a little seedy and potentially dangerous. The time I was able to walk to the bank coincided with the time when the only other people out on the street were the homeless, jobless, and fearless. As a result, I was mugged by a young punk who pulled a knife on me. Fortunately, I got away after giving him five bucks.

Never made it to the bank that day, but we got the mortgage later anyway.

When I returned to my office, the adrenaline still coursing, I composed a letter to my company's CEO. I explained what happened to me that morning, my concern for other employees facing the same hazards, and my willingness to volunteer to serve on a company committee to address this problem on behalf of all downtown workers. After that, I felt a little better, having made my CEO aware of an issue affecting his employees and offering to be a part of the solution.

About three days later, my immediate supervisor called me into his office, and he didn't look very happy. He asked if I had sent a letter to the CEO about being mugged, which I acknowledged. Then he said he just got off the phone with the CEO, who reamed him out something fierce. Dumbfounded, I asked what was the problem? And my boss said that the CEO had told him, "Your employee should have known better, especially coming from Corporate Communications!"

The real issue came down to the CEO not feeling as though he needed to interact with—or even hear directly from—someone like me so far down the totem pole. He thought I should have pushed the message up through channels, and not started at the top.

That kind of thinking sounded like nonsense to me then, and it still does. What's worse, too many CEOs still think that way. Take the recent case of an AT&T Wireless customer sending two e-mails directly to CEO Randall Stephenson, the first asking if his eligibility date for a discounted phone upgrade could moved up in time for the expected next-generation iPhone, and the second registering a complaint about the phase-out of unlimited data plans. Nothing threatening or untoward—just a customer going straight to the top for answers.

AT&T Wireless' immediate reaction? A voicemail message from the company's Orwellian-sounding "executive response team" thanking him "for the feedback" then following up with a warning: "If you continue to send e-mails to Randall Stephenson, a cease-and-desist letter may be sent to you."

Reach out and squash someone. Beautiful, AT&T Wireless. Just beautiful.

The company later apologized, saying the incident does not reflect on how it wants to treat its customers, yadda, yadda, yadda. I think old Randall has been sniffing the rarefied air on the C-Suite a little too long, and forgets who pays his salary—the little schlub nobodies like me and you and this e-mailing customer who got swatted like a pesky mosquito.

When Dorothy and her Yellow Brick Road pals tried to get in to see the Wizard of Oz, the guard's hysterical response was, "Nobody gets to see the Great Oz, not nobody, not no how!" It sounded dumb in the movies, and it sounds even dumber in real life.

CEOs of the world, get over yourselves. Take a page from Apple's CEO Steve Jobs, who somehow responds to every e-mail he receives. There are many reasons his company is admired, and that's got to be a big one.

Discussion Prompts:

1. What do you think would cause a typical consumer to try to communicate directly with a corporate CEO? What outcomes would that person be expecting?
2. Why do you think a CEO would establish a policy either in support of or in opposition to responding to these types of direct outreach?
3. What would be your advice to a CEO in making this decision, if you were in charge of communications for the organization? Why?

Chapter 4
DELIVERY

With leadership credentials established, a communications strategy in place, and the proper messaging developed, the final step in superior leadership communication comes in the delivery.

Here's where all of the thinking, analysis, reasoning, writing and preparation either pays off or not. A pitcher may have a blazing fastball, killer curve, and awesome slider, but if he never throws the ball toward home plate, what good is all that latent talent?

Many of the essays in this chapter deal with effective speechgiving delivery, and that's important since the act of public speaking is proven to be perhaps the most effective way to communicate ideas to large numbers of people. Issuing written documents certainly works, as well, but there's something innately captivating and more easily and deeply retainable about the spoken word.

My fellow presenters at speechwriting panel discussion at George Washington University came from governmental agencies for the most part, whereas my experience has been in the world of business. It didn't really seem to matter all that much, though, because we all—once it was our turn to take the stage—soon got so involved in our remarks that the audience of about 100 or so novice speechwriters got swept up into our enthusiasm, as well.

Why is that? Why such energy and—dare I say it—joy in this form of communication? While I would not pretend to speak for my compatriots in the speechwriting brother- and sister-hood, I know why I have such passion for this practice. It's something very simple, but very heartfelt. It's the privilege of playing such a critical role in helping CEOs and other leaders effectively and memorably convey the thoughts, hopes and plans they carry in their heads and hearts for the people they lead.

The right words indeed matter. The right words spur action. The right words make a difference and lead to growth, success, and fulfillment. Speechwriters get to write those words. It is an honor and, yes, a joy. Yet the real power comes when those words are delivered with confidence, command, and control.

It's all in the delivery, as the essays to follow demonstrate.

4.1
Mrs. Hesselbein, Spellbinder

The Big Idea: The first 60 seconds spell success or failure for a speaker.

> *"Spanning the globe...*
> *to bring you the constant variety of sport.*
> *The thrill of victory...and the agony of defeat.*
> *The human drama of athletic competition.*
> *This is ABC's Wide World of Sports."*

When I heard Jim McKay intone those words, with that wonderfully emotive music behind him, my heartbeat quickened. Something great and different and interesting was headed my way via the big Sears console in our living room, all those years ago.

A great opening makes all the difference. The same goes for a speech. If I had to guess, I'd say about 99.9999 percent of all speakers begin by thanking a dozen people, saying rather unconvincingly what a thrill/honor/pleasure it is to be here, blah, blah, blah.

This becomes a time for the audience to mentally go for a little walk, thinking about how cold the mashed potatoes were, or wondering how long this speech will last, or whether they remembered to unplug the hair dryer that morning. The audience can afford to take this cerebral stroll because none of what the speaker's saying means a thing.

The point of a speech, after all, is to present fresh information that piques the curiosity, startles the intellect, shakes the assumptions, and redirects the thinking of the audience. Why not get to the good stuff right away? Or at least grab their attention?

One of the best openings to a speech I ever experienced occurred at a conference about a year ago. Frances Hesselbein, winner of the Presidential Medal of Freedom for her lifetime of excellence in public service and non-profit leadership, was at the lectern. Mrs. Hesselbein is a petite, extremely graceful and gracious lady. She exudes dignity, a quiet confidence, and the respect earned from decades of outstanding achievement.

After she had been introduced, she walked to the microphone without notes. She did not speak immediately, but smiled and looked all around the packed ballroom before her, taking in as many eyes as she could. The effect was mesmerizing. She was building an incredible rapport with hundreds of individuals without saying a word. The room became absolutely silent, but not uncomfortably so. Rather, the feeling, the unexpressed wish coursing through the audience, was an almost unbearable expectation. Mrs. Hesselbein had us in the palm of her hand, and we had yet to hear her voice.

At last, she closed her eyes for a moment, looked up and smiled at all of us again, leaned into the microphone and spoke in a whisper, "I'd like to share a story with you."

For the next 30 minutes, she could have read us the Yellow Pages and it wouldn't have mattered. Her patience, grace, warmth, nonverbal engagement, and yeah I'll admit it—her complete playing of us like a cheap fiddle—worked like no other opening I've ever witnessed.

This of course isn't the only way to grab an audience right off the bat. You can say something totally unexpected, like the commencement speech I wrote for an executive, where the first two words were, "Get out!"

Or you can make a bold declaration, like the time I had a client open his speech with, "Nobody in Washington knows what they're doing."

Or you can even start off using a prop, like the time my client started popping plastic bubble wrap before the first words were uttered.

Each of these openings had a purpose, by the way. Being different without a point is, well, pointless.

Ditch the usual thank-yous and statements of humility. All of that's assumed. Don't give your audience a chance to go for a mental stroll. They may not come back. Take a cue from Mrs. Hesselbein, that accomplished spellbinder. Get the audience to focus on you, then get to the good stuff right away.

Discussion Prompts:

1. Can you think of a colorful opening to a speech that you've heard?
2. Explain why it was effective.
3. Write an opening to a speech about your career. What would grab your audience's attention or pique their curiosity?

4.2
All I Really Needed to Know I Learned Watching 'Seinfeld'
The Big Idea: The best speakers use every tool available.

You've heard of these books. "All I Really Needed to Know I Learned in Kindergarten." "The Seven Habits of Highly Successful People." "Good to Great." A stroll down the self-help aisle at any chain bookstore offers scores of similar titles.

But I've found some of the greatest tips not in the pages of a book, but on a treasured set of DVDs—the entire "Seinfeld" collection. And it's my pleasure to share some of those pointers, especially as they pertain to making successful public presentations.

First, there's the instance of the "low talker," Kramer's fashion designer date, who got Jerry to agree to wear the "puffy shirt" on the Today Show. Only problem was, she spoke so softly that Jerry and Elaine really didn't hear her make the request, so they just nodded in the affirmative so as to not appear rude.

Lesson learned for anyone speaking to a group? Open your mouth! Make your jaw go wide. Stretch your facial muscles before you get up to speak. And while you're making your presentation, keep the flow of air wide and open from your diaphragm and out past your teeth. The audience is there to hear you, so you are obligated to honor that expectation.

Then there's the "close talker," Elaine's friend who would stand uncomfortably close to anyone with whom he was speaking. I call this the "Wanting It Too Much" syndrome for speakers who like to escape from the podium and prowl into an audience. An eagerness to connect on a personal level is great, but bursting through people's individual bubble space actually has the opposite effect and repels those you're trying to embrace.

Lesson learned? Use vocal inflections, warm eye contact, and genuine gestures to engage the audience. Again, they're eager to connect with you too. They just don't want to go steady on the first date, so attempting a physical closeness is uncomfortable, unnatural, and unnecessary.

And lastly comes Kramer's big break when he's cast in a Woody Allen movie being filmed in Manhattan. As he tries to find just the right delivery for his single line of dialogue, "These pretzels are making me thirsty," this simple statement gets repeated by virtually everyone in the episode in different contexts, with wildly varying intonations and meanings.

Lesson learned? A well-crafted presentation has intentional phrasing, pauses, passages meant to be spoken softly, verbal crescendos leading to major payoff declarations, and many more verbal cues. The great speakers look for these opportunities to maximize the impact of their delivery for their audiences, and rehearse ahead of time to find just the right blend of information, entertainment, humor, and drama.

Now, if you'll excuse me, I need to pour myself a tall glass of iced tea. These pretzels are making me thirsty.

Discussion Prompts:

1. Watch videos of John F. Kennedy's Inaugural Address from Jan. 20, 1961, and Jimmy Carter's Inaugural Address from Jan. 20, 1977 (both available on YouTube).
2. Describe the differences between the two speeches in terms of energy, vocabulary used, elegance of phrasing, and any other rhetorical measurements that strike you.

4.3

The Incredible Mr. Vis

The Big Idea: Face-to-face communication remains the most powerful form.

The year was 1970 and I was all of 10 years old, one of about 40 Cub Scouts sitting on the floor of the local Moose Lodge one chilly Friday evening, held captive by the superlative storytelling of Mr. Vis, one of the troop leaders.

Good gravy, Mr. Vis knew how to spin a tale. Using only his voice and his gestures, he had us Scouts (and our parents) alternatingly in terror or in stitches, crawling through a murky forest or soaring through a golden cloud, taking on a gang of villains or taking off for a new adventure. He did it with such aplomb, zest, and joy, that 40 years later I can still conjure the experience clearly in my mind.

Faxes didn't exist back then. No e-mail either. Texting, Facebook, Twitter, or any of the other electronic means to communicate we enjoy (or is it endure?) today would have fallen under the rubric of science fiction when Nixon occupied the White House. Nope, we had the U.S. Postal Service, the Bell Telephone Company, and each other. Those were pretty much the only means of communication.

And I miss those days.

According to a study done by GfK Technology cited in Fortune for Small Business magazine, 87 percent of adults today say they prefer dealing with others in person instead of via computers or smartphones. The same compilation of statistics shows that, according to Pear Analytics, 62 percent of all Tweets comprise babble or otherwise worthless information.

Of course, social media is here to stay, yet so much of it seems trivial, impersonal, and actually uncommunicative to me. Why does the English language need to fit on a two-inch screen? My guess is that most people have first-hand experience of an e-mail or text message—especially one meant to be funny or sarcastic—being misinterpreted and requiring even more follow-up damage-control communications. That's silly and such a waste of time.

When you're speaking on the phone, or better yet face-to-face with someone, the chances of being properly understood would seem to increase exponentially. When people can hear vocal inflections, read facial expressions, and get a human feel for what's being said, things just work out better.

As a professional writer, I also get concerned about the ability of people to communicate powerful ideas with passion, to build and utilize a robust vocabulary, and to sustain a cogent thought for at least a paragraph or two. Anyone who thinks Tweeting will help along those lines qualifies as a twit in my book.

I overhear young people in my neighborhood debating ways to communicate with their friends, but placing a phone call where they would actually have to speak back and forth with another person rarely even gets considered. That's a damn shame. My bet is, if kids today had been with me and my friends as Mr. Vis wove his amazing stories, they'd feel differently and would look for ways to talk face-to-face more often.

Discussion Prompts:

1. Choose a day to conduct a personal experiment. See if you can go 12 straight hours by only speaking directly to other people, either in person or by phone. No texts, Tweets, Facebook, or any other electronic means are permitted.
2. Describe the experiment and what you might have learned or observed about communication as a result.

4.4
Stop, Forrest, Stop!

The Big Idea: Knowing when to finish is as important as anything you say.

The classic film "Forrest Gump" features a funny scene where one portion of the student body at the University of Alabama holds up placards in the stands that read "RUN FORREST RUN" as the dim-witted but fleet-footed Gump rumbles downfield to score a touchdown, while the placards of another student section facing the end zone read "STOP" to make sure he doesn't run straight out of the stadium.

I find that scene funny because there are times I wish I had some "STOP" placards in my briefcase when people really just need to cease talking and sit down. And the list starts with me, some 25 years ago.

My first job in public relations came as an assistant spokesperson for a district of the Pennsylvania Department of Transportation. After a public meeting about a new highway interchange, I was interviewed by the local TV stations.

"Answer the question, then stop talking," my boss had advised me earlier. But when you're 24 years old, inexperienced, nervous, staring down the barrel of a video camera, and eager to be helpful, that advice somehow gets filed in the wrong drawer in your brain. Oh, I answered the questions all right, along with sharing lots of un-asked-for-but-eagerly-recorded thoughts about the project, the quality of comments received at the meeting, and more.

The next morning I showed up for work looking like a puppy that got into the garbage can and had strewn refuse all over the house. I just didn't know when to shut up. It's an affliction that touches millions daily in all walks of life, but I'm most interested when it strikes people who ought to know better.

Motivational speakers who have so many good stories, yet feel compelled to tell them all. Preachers who have the gift of stringing together inspiring words, yet never seem to run out of string. Elected officials who deal with weighty issues every day, yet assume that we're as interested as they are. Business leaders who know all there is to know about their company, yet can't stop themselves from expounding on things they don't know as well.

Here's the concept in a nutshell: Think about what you're trying to communicate. Get it all down on paper. Organize it into a logical flow. State your main point then cite supporting information until that same point becomes as clear as possible. Edit it down. Then edit it down again. Then think some more and edit it down again.

What you're left with is a well-reasoned document that should convey your message with a clarity and crispness that's easy to understand. It provides the basis for effective verbal communication, as well, whether in a formal presentation or in handling interviews.

Today when I speak to groups, the first thing I say is, "As the speaker, it's my job to speak. As the audience, it's your job to listen. I will do my best to finish my job before you finish yours." That usually does the trick, keeping me honest and forcing me to be as succinct as possible while never shortchanging the audience's expectations or their due.

In other words, you have to know when to stop, Forrest, stop.

Discussion Prompts:
Reporters try to get subjects to say more than they had planned. List three ways to keep yourself or your client from falling into this trap.

4.5

The Delicate Art of the Eulogy

The Big Idea: There is no greater honor and no tougher assignment than a eulogy.

A great friend recently had the heavy honor of delivering the eulogy for a family member, and asked me for some guidance. My advice was brief and direct: "A eulogy is no time to scrimp on the superlatives," and, "Pick a spot above people's heads to focus on, or otherwise you may not get through it." Unfortunately, I knew the value of that advice from a number of first-hand experiences.

Crafting a eulogy is unlike any other form of speechwriting. It must be respectful but not cold, insightful but not intrusive, emotional but not exploitative. Its delivery requires an enormous level of internal strength and focus, but with enough shared feeling to truly honor the person being celebrated.

One of the greatest challenges of my professional career came when six employees of the company I worked for were lost in an airplane crash, and it fell to me to write the entire script for a memorial service to be attended by the victims' families and company employees. Simple, heartfelt, hopeful language containing specific references to each victim's personal and professional lives carried the day, but getting to that point just about took everything out of me.

That artful blending of simplicity of feeling, heartfelt emotion, and hopeful inspiration marks the great eulogies, and we will hear more of this during the memorial services for Sen. Edward Kennedy this weekend. Here are just a few examples of stirring eulogies from recent memory:

"Above all we give thanks for the life of a woman I am so proud to be able to call my sister—the unique, the complex, the extraordinary and irreplaceable Diana, whose beauty, both internal and external, will never be extinguished from our minds."

- From the eulogy for Princess Diana by her brother Charles Spencer, September 1997

"And as the last journey of this faithful pilgrim took him beyond the sunset, and as heaven's morning broke, I like to think—in the words of Bunyan—that `all the trumpets sounded on the other side.'"
- From the eulogy for President Ronald Reagan by former British Prime Minister Margaret Thatcher, June 2004

"Like the sun, she bathed us in her warm glow. Now that the sun has set and the cool of the evening has come, some of the warmth we absorbed is flowing back towards her."
- From the eulogy for the Queen Mother by the Archbishop of Canterbury, Dr. George Carey, April 2002

"He was lost on that troubled night, but we will always wake for him, so that his time, which was not doubled, but cut in half, will live forever in our memory, and in our beguiled and broken hearts. We dared to think, in that other Irish phrase, that this John Kennedy would live to comb gray hair, with his beloved Carolyn by his side. But like his father, he had every gift but length of years."
- From the eulogy for John F. Kennedy Jr. by Sen. Edward Kennedy, July 1999

Writing and delivering eulogies is indeed a heavy honor, but one that should be embraced for the truly unique and incredibly wonderful chance to commemorate and celebrate the richness and reward of an individual's life.

Discussion Prompts:

1. Delivering a tribute to someone special requires great self-control. If you have ever heard a eulogy delivered live, what do you think the speaker was thinking and feeling during his or her remarks?
2. How well did the speaker meet his or her obligation? Why?

4.6

Open Mouth, Insert Cleats

The Big Idea: Hard as it may be, one must remain alert when talking to the media.

It's tough to appreciate it until you're actually in the moment, but there's a world of difference between standing up on short notice to speak before a group, and handling an impromptu news conference.

Most noticeably, when you're at a podium, you're in control of the environment, the pace, and the content of what is said—but while during a news conference with microphones suddenly in your face, the reporter is in control and you're forced to react and play defense.

Part of my practice is dedicated to helping clients get ready for either situation, and there are plenty of examples of folks fumbling the ball. Try these verbal clunkers on for size, all from the wide world of sports:

- "Nobody in football should be called a genius. A genius is a guy like Norman Einstein." This gem comes to us from Washington Redskins quarterback and Notre Dame alumnus Joe Theismann. Somewhere, Knute Rockne is weeping.

- George Foreman, in his pre-grill boxing days, once quipped: "The referee is the most important man in the ring besides the two fighters." Well, I guess that narrows it down.

- Torrin Polk, who toiled as a wide receiver at the University of Houston, once boasted of his head coach, "He treats us like men. He lets us wear earrings." Coach must have drawn the line at wearing open-toed pumps with cleats, though.

- "I owe a lot to my parents, especially my mother and father," said golfer and aspiring genealogist Greg Norman.

- Here's one from way back, attributed to Ohio State quarterback Bob Hoying: "I'm really happy for Coach Cooper and the guys who've been around here for six or seven years, especially our seniors." And here, all this time, I thought they called it the Big Ten because of the number of teams in the conference, not the years required to graduate.

- "Hawaii doesn't win many games in the United States," opined Lee Corso, former college coach, current ESPN football analyst, and quite possibly the first guy to sit down during every geography bee he's ever entered.

Again, to be fair, it takes real concentration in the heat of the moment to calm the mind sufficiently, so that only cogent statements come out of one's mouth. For athletes and other performers in particular, the surge of adrenalin can addle the brain cells a bit, leading to some of the bloopers cited above.

As with anything else in communications, preparation, practice and persistence are invaluable. Making the sort of humorous statements seen here can be charming and endearing. You just don't want to make a habit of it.

Discussion Prompts:

1. Pick a news or sports story from today's news, read it, become an expert on it.
2. Stand at a podium and field questions from others in your group.
3. List three rules for properly handling media questions that you gleaned from this experience.

4.7

You Can't Fake Sincerity, and Only Fools Try

The Big Idea: Memorable speeches are marked by the speaker's passion.

On a sun-splashed June 12, 1987, the President of the United States stood at a microphone in front of the Brandenburg Gate in what was then known as West Berlin. His words that day shook the world.

What few people realize is that Ronald Reagan's prepared remarks that day only read, "Mr. Gorbachev, open this gate." The President wrote the next line on his own, the line that electrified the crowd and hastened the collapse of the Soviet Union and the eventual reunification of Germany some two and a half years later: ***"Mr. Gorbachev, tear down this wall!"***

When you hear the force behind Reagan's declaration, the emphatic emotion behind the first word of that phrase, ***"TEAR—*** down—this—wall!" there is no disputing the fact that he believed in what he was saying. He absolutely meant it. He infused into that single sentence a quarter-century of frustration, anger, and disgust for what the Soviets had caused to the people of East Germany by building the Berlin Wall.

The tone of voice that leaders use when they speak before audiences carries more weight than they sometimes realize. An audience isn't stupid. People can tell whether a leader truly believes in what he or she is saying. You can't fake sincerity. Those who try may succeed for a time, but eventually the charade gets exposed and you're left with a shredded reputation. It's awfully tough to lead effectively once that's happened.

As I work with client leaders to craft their messages and coach them on presenting those ideas with energy and passion, the first question I ask is, "If you were hearing this material for the first time, would you believe it and act on it?" If the answer is no, then we keep working.

Believing in what you say must be the foundation of communication. Anything less insults and shortchanges your audience, delays progress for your organization, and harms your ability to lead. Carrying forward a message that rings true in your own mind and heart stands at the center of meaningful communication and at the base of every effective leader, whether in politics or business.

Discussion Prompts:

1. Print out a CEO speech from the Investor Relations tab on a publicly held company's website. Read the script and mark it up, highlighting words the speaker should emphasize, places where the speaker should pause, etc.
2. Read aloud a key passage from your marked-up speech in two ways: first, with no vocal inflection at all; and second, using all of the markings you provided.
3. Evaluate the difference between the two approaches.

4.8
Rusty Clunker in the Fast Lane
The Big Idea: Play to your strengths as a speaker.

So I'm driving into Downtown Pittsburgh the other day for a client meeting, on a highway with a 55 mph speed limit. There's lots of traffic for some reason and it's tough to change lanes or get ahead of anybody—and then I see why.

Moseying along in the passing lane is a rusty old pickup truck with city Water and Sewer markings on it, the left turn signal lazily blinking, mile after mile, the driver ignorantly, blissfully oblivious to both the safety hazard and the traffic backup his little 40 mph joyride was creating. The only guy on the road in absolutely no hurry.

The wrong approach, the wrong time, and everybody else suffers.

Part of my practice occasionally requires that I save clients from themselves, to keep them from taking a wrong approach at the wrong time, and averting a situation where others suffer because of mistakes they might make. Case in point—the assumption that every speech has to open with a joke.

Let's face it, not everybody's Jerry Seinfeld or Jerry Lewis. Most business people in front of a group can barely muster Jerry Van Dyke. Just because a CEO can crack up his executive staff at the Monday morning meeting doesn't mean he's ready for Open Mike Night at the Improv.

I much prefer arming my clients with gentle self-deprecating openings like, "I promise to not make this a Texas longhorn speech—you know, a point here, a point there, and a lot of bull in between." Going for the big laugh cuts both ways, you can either bring down the house or bring down the curtain even before the show really starts. Most times, it's just too risky.

Another case in point—the fear of being bold. A speaker typically is asked to appear before a group because he has a unique perspective, a history of expertise, or a wealth of knowledge on a topic that the host wants to learn more about. When you are at the microphone, you are in command. Everyone is eager to hear what you have to say. Polluting your comments with a lot of hedging, halting, hesitating language like, "I think" or "It may be the case" or "Perhaps we can say" is just plain gutless in my book.

Instead, once the material has been vetted and validated, have the bones to make declarative statements, to convey true belief in what you're communicating so that your audience believes it and, more important, believes you. "We know" and "Undoubtedly" and "It has been proven that" beats the wishy-washy stuff any day of the week.

An audience wants to be moved. To get somewhere new through a speaker's words and thoughts. It's my joy as a speechwriter and presentation coach to help clients achieve those objectives for their audiences when they step to the podium—and to not be the rusty clunker in the fast lane, holding everybody else up.

Discussion Prompts:

1. Watch a speaker on YouTube or C-SPAN and get a sense of how bold the language used is.
2. Describe your impressions and any suggestions on how to make those remarks more declarative and definitive.

4.9
Nobody Likes Charades Anyway
The Big Idea: Be yourself.

A friend recently asked how I might go about training exec-utives from India on making effective presentations to American audiences. My reply was simple, direct, and automatic—help them become as confident, comfortable, and in command of their material as possible, and most of all don't try to turn them into something or someone they're not.

History is replete with speakers making spectacular fools of themselves by putting on personas that fit like hot pants on a rhi-noceros. As a professional speechwriter, I know that developing a great speech requires both science and art. The "science" en-tails developing a central theme, a compelling argument, and the documentation and supporting facts to give that argument validity. The "art," on the other hand, means weaving all of those facts and arguments and statements into a conversational nar-rative using vocabulary and phrasing that naturally sounds like the way the speaker typically communicates.

Why are both elements important? Because if an audi-ence can sense that the speaker is the least bit uncomfortable or awkward with the words being spoken, then it's no longer a speech—it's a research paper standing on its hind legs.

Occasionally the cosmic tumblers all click into place and a speaker can rise above himself to greater rhetorical heights, but only occasionally. As a famous recent example, President George W. Bush simply was not built to use soaring rhetoric for the sake of soaring rhetoric. Yet in his speech to a joint session of Congress on Sept. 20, 2001, following the terrorist attacks on the U.S., his language was elevated, inspirational, infused with pas-sion, righteous anger, and national pride—and it worked beauti-fully.

Why? Because he believed it, he held the required convic-tion in his bones and it came through in his delivery. It was the greatest speech of his presidency and he rarely, if ever, matched the rhetorical heights of that moment. If anything, to his detractors, he soon slipped too well and too comfortably into his own unique form of Texas patter and never quite captured the national soul in his words the same way again.

Like the articulate but homely Cyrano de Bergerac providing the simple-minded fraud Christian with lines of romance to the lovely Roxane, the charade of trying to be someone you're not can't last for long. In the story, Christian gets shot, Roxane enters a convent, and Cyrano takes a log to the noggin and dies. I'm proud to report that none of those things have ever happened to my clients—because I never coach them to be anything than what they are, other than a more confident version.

At its core, great speakers—and great speech coaching— must center on three things:
1.   Confidence, or the speaker's belief that he's ready to be in front of an audience.
2.   Comfort, or the speaker's belief that he likes being there.
3.   Command, or the speaker's belief that he's helping everyone in the room be happy that he's up there, too.

And rule number one is, don't try to be something or someone you're not. Nobody likes to play charades anyway.

Discussion Prompts:
1.   **Why do you think people try to "be someone else" when they speak in public?**
2.   **What effect can that approach have on an audience?**
3.   **How would you advise a speaker to overcome this tendency?**

4.10
Listen to Your Stink-O-Meter
The Big Idea: If you see a problem, address it quickly.

There ain't no such thing as a sure thing. One very painful afternoon in a hotel ballroom proved that to me.

Back when I was part of the internal communications staff at a major corporation, my duties included organizing an annual luncheon to kick off the region's U.S. Savings Bond sales campaign. This entailed a number of tasks, with securing a dynamite keynote speaker being the most important.

Working with my company's on-call public relations agency, we brainstormed ideas concerning what we wanted in our keynoter. This person needed to exude energy, to feel passionately about things, and most of all, had to establish and maintain a level of interest among a room full of 250 people after they've consumed a midday chicken-and-mashed potatoes meal.

Lucky for us, we found the perfect guy. A sure thing. A lock. You can figure out where this story is headed from here.

This fellow was one of the assistant coaches for our town's NFL team. His antics during each week's game had become legendary. He ran the length of the field, it seemed, each time his players took to the gridiron. He jumped in the air. He hugged his guys, he shouted and celebrated along with them. He had an electricity about him that appeared to be contagious. He'd be a powerhouse speaker. Or so we thought.

We called the team and booked him for the big date, sight unseen. Hence, I refer to this episode as one of my Legendary Rookie Mistakes.

The day of the luncheon, I greeted our keynote speaker before the event began, thanking him in advance for his help. He acknowledged my greeting, but something looked a little off. His eyes darted like tiny black pinballs. He looked a tad sweaty. His suit hung from his frame uncomfortably. None of this bothered me at the time, unfortunately. My Stink-O-Meter should have been shrieking, as it would today. But when you're a rookie, well, that's what makes you a rookie.

My company's top regional executive served as the emcee, and once all the opening pleasantries had been taken care of, lunch was served. My cohort from the PR agency and I glanced at each other, silently patting ourselves on the back for the spectacularness to come. At last, the moment arrived. The emcee read the introduction I had written for the keynoter, building expectations that not even Tony Robbins, Bill Clinton, and Knute Rockne—put together—could meet. Looking back, it really was unfair to everyone in the room.

Our man took the podium and, God bless him, dived in. Forty-five excruciating minutes later, he finished. The room held an atmosphere of stunned relief, odd bewilderment, and simmering anger—almost like, "We're so unbelievably glad that's over and we'd like to stay just a few minutes longer and strangle whoever picked this guy as keynote speaker."

Not to exaggerate, mind you.

The big lesson learned that day? Trust your gut, but verify what it's telling you. We should have insisted on tapes of our candidate making presentations at other venues. We should have done our homework a lot better. All the things I know to do today. Cause there ain't no such thing as a sure thing. Your Stink-O-Meter knows. Listen to it.

Discussion Prompts:
People forget about the importance and the opportunity afforded by a well-written speaker introduction. Select a person you know and write a colorful, interesting, and factually accurate introduction about them—making sure that it positions them properly and sets suitable audience expectations.

4.11
I Like Facebook, HBU (how 'bout you)?
The Big Idea: It's important to stay abreast of new tools and vocabulary.

As a newbie to Facebook, I'm in the process of learning not only how to navigate these new waters of Walls and Friending and feigning interest in people's toenail painting appointments, but also how to communicate business opportunities to heretofore untapped markets.

The universe of Twitter beckons as well, but my limit is one culture shock at a time, thanks.

One of the more fascinating aspects of these and other social media is the quicksilver development of language and novel abbreviations. With three teenagers in the house, the fact that this is happening comes as no surprise. Yet the sheer volume of newly hatched acronyms, homonyms, and synonyms leaves me speechless. And I'm a speechwriter, 4COL (for crying out loud).

As a parent, I want to know what the kids are talking about out there to keep mine safe. As a professional communicator, I want to know what language usages the world is embracing to keep my clients informed and protected, as well. A recent article in The Wall Street Journal gives a very informed and informative rundown of this constantly evolving vocabulary, and quotes a media trainer as stating, "If a CEO does not appear to be tech-savvy, people may start to wonder, 'Is the company not plugged into today's technologies also?'"

I'm not sure the thumbs of CEOs with whom I work are furiously flurrying over their Blackberrys and iPhones with gems like KUTGW (keep up the good work), WRUD (what are you doing), or GBTW (get back to work). Well, maybe that last one. But the notion of remaining tech-savvy does ring true.

The only thing that never changes is the fact that everything changes. Social media drives presidential politics, athletes bypassing the media and going straight to their fan base, heck, even Paula Abdul resigned from "American Idol" via Twitter. What more proof does anyone need?

For now, I plan to dive back into my Facebook account and start swimming again, looking for fresh Friends who can lead me to vast new worlds of business connections. My message to them? PCM (please call me).

Discussion Prompts:
Perform a self-evaluation of your Facebook page to look for any embarrassing or questionable messages, videos or photos. Human Resources managers and other hiring officers will look at your social media history before seriously considering you for job openings.

4.12
Tire-Tread Graffiti: The Mess That Lasts

The Big Idea: Leaders should expect more of themselves as communicators.

They painted a brand new double-yellow line down the center of the main road near my house last week. It must have looked so pristine, so clean and neat, the two parallel stripes of paint telling drivers to stay on their side of the road.

I say it "must have" because the first time I saw it, some knucklehead had intentionally zig-zagged his car across the wet paint about six times, spewing a trail of yellow tire-tread marks all over the road—a complete eyesore that my neighbors and I will be forced to look at and live with for the next five years until the municipality paints the lines again.

If there isn't a crime on the books for "tire-tread graffiti," may I be the first to suggest one? Never fear, dear readers, there is a parallel in the world of executive communications. It's the dragging along of bad habits that hinder and hurt the potential of leaders to truly stir the people and organizations they hope to lead. Here are some examples of "tire-tread graffiti" I run up against all too often:

- *A refusal to rehearse a speech out loud before standing behind the lectern.* Having a thousand eyeballs staring at you is hardly the time to be considering a speech seriously for the first time. A well-crafted presentation deserves your attention well ahead of that moment of truth. What's more, your audience deserves your best effort—and that includes rehearsing the speech aloud and accepting coaching to maximize your delivery.

- *An insistence on stressing multiple "very important" topics in a single speech.* Here's a good rule of thumb I remind my clients of every now and then—when everything's important, nothing is. To the irritation of the occasional executive, I insist on identifying what I call the "Sunrise Statement"—the single idea that an audience member can cite when asked the next day, "What did that person talk about?" While an internal audience may be able to absorb a lot of different topics, with equal weight assigned to each, an external audience would only become confused and disengaged. Again, the audience deserves to be respected by keeping the messaging clear and focused.

- *An over-reliance on PowerPoint.* The human brain can only handle one task at a time. When a speaker uses 50 images in a 20-minute talk, I see that as a problem. When most of those images are chock-full of charts and text, I see that as a joke. I once saw a CFO at an annual meeting of shareholders use a slide that had so much on it that part of the words actually spilled over onto the draping around the projection screen. Ludicrous! By doing this, you're inviting the audience to stop listening to you, because they're so preoccupied reading and trying to make sense of the blizzard of words and numbers before their eyes. It's a speech, folks. It's meant to be heard. By human ears. Images that support what's being spoken? Great. Charts that show general trends? Yep. But keep them simple, so the audience always chooses to listen to you over reading the slides.

Years ago, when I was on the payroll of some large corporations, making these observations and suggestions could be difficult. As an outside consultant I'm not really that much smarter, but somehow clients are more apt to listen. That's a tremendous perk to my chosen profession, because rooting out and changing these bad habits helps executives become better communicators, which only helps their organizations. Otherwise, these types of "tire-tread graffiti" just keep making messes that last.

Discussion Prompts:
Go this site: <u>http://norvig.com/Gettysburg/sld002.htm</u>. There is nothing more to be said about how ridiculous and unnecessary PowerPoint can be.

CONCLUSION

True leaders are good communicators. They don't need to be great, simply being good puts them ahead of their counterparts by leaps and bounds. And it's not that difficult to get to good.

As the stories I've shared in this book prove over and over again, good leadership communication is all too often a case of simple common sense. If a leader gives communication as high a priority as his or her other key objectives, the picture becomes clear very quickly—when you communicate well with your people, your ability to lead gets easier and more effective because you have followers who understand your vision and who want to contribute toward achieving it.

The first step is accepting the mantle of leadership itself. You are in charge. People are looking to you for direction, guidance, direction, and inspiration. Only by you communicating effectively can they get these vital sets of information. Get close to your people, let them see you. Encourage two-way dialogue and live up to that promise. Trust provides the basis for credibility and acceptance, so use regular communications to build that base of trust.

Next comes a strategic approach. By understanding what your communication efforts are meant to do in pursuit of your vision for the organization, the execution of those efforts can be planned, tracked, and measured effectively. But again, any strategy must take into consideration the perspective, level of understanding, and beliefs of the people you're hoping to lead. Knowing your audience and working in alignment with their attributes helps feed into development of any solid communications strategy.

Messaging is where the strategy begins to take tangible shape. Bridging the gap between your vision and the point of view of your people requires careful attention to how your messages are crafted. Inspirational, yet relatable. Challenging, yet positive. Motivational, yet reassuring. It's not always an easy balance, but when done properly it can change the destiny of an organization positively for years.

And finally comes delivery. You have accepted your role as leader. You have a communications strategy in place. Your messages have been crafted carefully and well. Now they must be delivered with passion, belief, energy, confidence, conviction, and a vision for the future. The best recipe for leaders in carrying out this final phase of a solid communications effort entails hard work to internalize the messages—to make them so ingrained in your mind and heart, that when you share them with your people there can be no doubt as to your veracity and sincerity.

Good leadership communication makes an enormous difference in morale, performance, and productivity. CEOs who regularly represent their organizations well through coordinated communications efforts can even help to positively influence stock price, according to a survey done a few years ago by the global communications firm Burson Marsteller.

In short, the last thing you want to be as a leader regarding your communications is helpless, clueless, hopeless, and friendless—like a jackass in a hailstorm. Come in from the rain and hail and wind. Sharpen that necktie knot. Take a look in the mirror and see a solid communicator, a terrific leader, looking back at you. Now go back out there and show them how it's done.

ABOUT THE AUTHOR

Tim Hayes brings nearly three decades of outstanding communications counsel and tactical experience—particularly at the leadership level—to clients. He shares much of that experience and lessons learned along the way in his first book, ***Jackass in a Hailstorm: Adventures in Leadership Communication.***

He has been named the No. 1 Speechwriter by the Washington, DC, chapter of the International Association of Business Communicators; winner of the top speech in the nation by PR News in its Platinum PR Awards; a national Cicero Speechwriting Award winner, and has been honored by more than 20 regional and state awards for excellence in writing. He is the subject of two USA Today articles, is a regular guest expert on regional and national radio programs, and has become recognized as a national resource regarding helping leaders perfect their public personas.

Since 2000, he has led Tim Hayes Consulting as president, working to effectively position organizations in the marketplace through intelligent, well-reasoned and well-crafted speechwriting, executive message development, employee programs, government relations support, technical writing and public relations.

Through his Total Pro line of services, Tim offers personalized leadership communications training at management retreats, conference appearances, and one-to-one consulting sessions.

Tim has served leaders of all types of organizations through annual reports, transparency and sustainability reports, strategic speechwriting and presentation coaching, employee communications efforts, and other high-level communications designed to achieve key business objectives.

Tim has worked directly with CEOs and other senior executives of major corporations, including Daimler-Chrysler, United States Steel Corp., H.J. Heinz Company, PNC Financial Services Group Inc., Mellon Financial Corp., GNC Inc., PPL Corporation, Grant Thornton LLC, Fleet Boston Corp., Highmark Blue Cross Blue Shield, Banco Santander Corp., Federated Investors Inc., Wabtec Inc., Michael Baker Corp., iGate Global Solutions Inc., Universal Stainless & Alloy Products Inc., Allegheny Ludlum Inc., Kennametal Inc., and the Pittsburgh Steelers.

His career began as a newspaper reporter, where he won a statewide award for news coverage of his alma mater, Indiana University of Pennsylvania. Tim earned a bachelor's degree in journalism from IUP in 1982. He resides with his family in suburban Pittsburgh, Pennsylvania.

www.timhayesconsulting.com
www.totalprotraining.com

Made in the USA
Charleston, SC
17 November 2010